INTERACTIONS

4

JACK HOPE   MARIAN SMALL
DALE DROST

Consultants

Valeen Chow
Ralph Connelly
Larry Elchuck
Peggy Hill
Deborah Tempest
Stella Tossell

ESL Consultant

Wendy McDonell

GINN

Ginn Publishing Canada Inc.

ISBN 0-7702-2351-6
C94043

PROGRAM MANAGER

Shirley Barrett

EDITORS

Janice Nixon
Lynda Cowan
Jane Hammond

ART/DESIGN

Sandi Meland Cherun/Word & Image Design Studio

ILLUSTRATORS

Steve Attoe
Steve Beinicke
Hélène Desputeaux
Mary Jane Gerber
Linda Hendry
Dan Hobbs
Tina Holdcroft
Vesna Krstanovich
Mike Martchenko
Louise Phillips
Scot Ritchie
Daniel Sylvestre

PHOTOGRAPHS

page 1, Comstock; page 31 top, Comstock/Pierre St. Jacques; page 31 bottom, Comstock/E. Otto; page 70, Comstock/Ron and Barb Kroll; page 232, Comstock/Harold M. Lambert

page 20 Tessa Macintosh/NWT

page 30, Unilock Ltd

page 86, Paolo Curto/Image Bank

page 175, Bettman Archives

page 179, Canapress

All product photos by Tom McCrae

All other photos by Ray Boudreau

Printed and bound in Canada
DEFG 9876

Table of Contents

Investigating Our Families

How might these people belong in family groups?
Does your family like having picnics? If so, how often?
How might you use mathematics in planning a picnic?

How Can We Describe Our Birthdays?

Cory and 7 classmates made a graph to show the birthdays for their families.

Our Families' Birthdays

January	6	17				
February	9	29	12	8		
March	15	21	3	31	17	
April	5	1	10	29	4	
May	22	19	3	16	12	3
June	7	4	23	30		
July						
August	15	14				
September	28	19	21	6		
October	11					
November	15					
December	24	31	8			

Each 🎂 stands for 1 birthday.
Numbers on the cakes show the days of the month.

1. Answer these questions about the graph.
   - Are half of the birthdays in the first half of the year?
   - How many birthdays are in each quarter of the year?
   - Does each season have the same number of birthdays?
   - Which birthdays are exactly 1 week apart?
   - Does the month before your birthday have more or fewer birthdays? How many?

   Now ask your own questions about the graph.

2

2. Find out the birthdays and years of birth for your family.
Would you expect more than 1 birthday in at least 1 month? Why?

3. Create a graph like Cory's for the families in your group.
Make up questions about your graph for another group to answer.

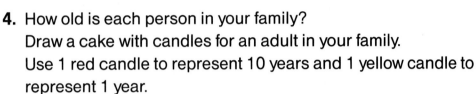

4. How old is each person in your family?
Draw a cake with candles for an adult in your family.
Use 1 red candle to represent 10 years and 1 yellow candle to represent 1 year.

5. What is your age in years, months, and days?
Are you more than 5000 days old?
Use a calculator to find out the exact number.

This poem might help you.

Thirty days have September,
April, June, and November.
All the rest have thirty-one,
Except February which has twenty-eight,
And leap year one in four
Gives it one more.

Did you know...?

In groups of 23 people, about half the groups will probably have 2 people with the same birthday.

▶ Investigate this for groups of 23.

Do you know anyone whose birthday is the same as yours?

HOW Many Times Do We Do Something?

Anya counted how many times her sister, brother, mother, uncle, and her dog, Duff, blinked in 1 minute.

Number of Blinks

Max	⫲⫲ ⫲⫲ ⫲⫲ ⫲⫲
Darla	⫲⫲ ‖
Mom	⫲⫲ ‖‖
Uncle	⫲⫲ ⫲⫲ ‖
Duff	‖‖

She used her tally chart to draw a pictograph.

	Blinks in 1 min
Max	👁 👁 👁 👁 👁 👁 👁 👁 👁 👁 👁
Darla	👁 👁 👁 ◖
Mom	👁 👁 👁 👁 ◖
Uncle	👁 👁 👁 👁 👁 👁
Duff	👁 ◖
Each 👁 stands for 2 blinks.	

1. What does half an eye represent in the pictograph?

2. Choose 2 members of Anya's family. What is the difference in the number of times they blinked? What do you think the reason might be?

3. Who do you think might blink the most in the next minute? Why? How many times do you think each member of Anya's family would blink in 5 min?

4

Joel counted the number of times his family said his name during dinner, then made a bar graph.

Saying "Joel"

A bar graph titled "Saying 'Joel'" with the y-axis labeled "Number of Times" from 0 to 10. The bars show: Dad = 5, Mom = 7, Grandma = 4, Hattie = 0, Brian = 2.

4. Tell why you think each person said Joel's name the number of times they did.

5. Do you think your name might be said during dinner the same number of times, more times, or fewer times than Joel's name was said? Why?

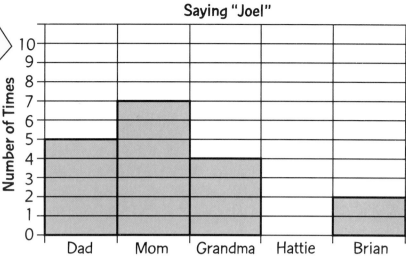

I wonder how many times each person in my home asks a question in a day.

Work with a partner.

6. Think of something to find out about both your families. Decide how long you will observe or listen.

I'd like to see how many times my family smiles in an hour.

7. Predict the number of times for each person in your own family. Then count the number of times.

8. Make a tally chart for your own family. Draw a pictograph or a bar graph for both families. Compare your graph with your predictions.

I want to know how many times people swallow in a minute.

I want to find out how many times each person in my family talks on the telephone in a week.

5

Name Puzzles

What letter in your name would you write last in
a 3 by 3 square?
a 4 by 4 square?
a 5 by 5 square?
How can you tell without writing the letters?
Try it with another name.

Pass the Floss!

Estimate the total length of
dental floss your family
should use in a year.
Is it more or less than 1 km?

Travelling to Work

How many kilometres has a family
member travelled to and from
work this year?

Don't Bounce

What is the largest family that
could fit in an elevator with a
capacity of 1000 kg?

Hair Today, Gone Tomorrow!

About how many haircuts
have the members of your
family had?

**Make up your OWN investigation.
Then post it on the bulletin board for
others to try.**

How do you think people in your family find out information?
What other ways would you suggest trying?

Tell how you could find out the number of times one person in your family walks through your front doorway in 1 week.

How might the number of times vary in different weeks and in different years?

What ways does your family use mathematics at home? away from home?

Create riddles like this about families.

Darin likes to visit his mother's mother. She's his _____?_____.

My stepfather's brother lives with us. He's my _____?_____.

What else would you like to know about families? Tell what you would do to find out.

Exploring

◄ How might the 3 children share the 7 cookies?

How might 3 children share 4 hamburgers?

How might they share 5 comic books?

How might the 4 children share the $3.00? ▶

How would you share this money fairly
with a friend?

How would you share *this* money fairly
with a friend?

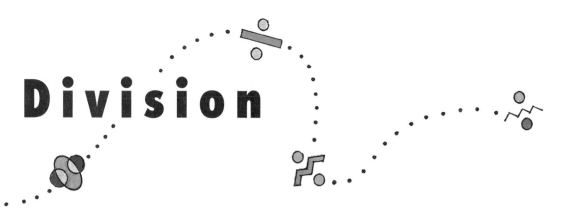

Division

▼ How would you place these 19 students in equal rows for their photo?

How would you seat 31 guests at 5 tables?

Write about a time when you shared things with other people.

Did every person get a fair share?

Estimate each total.

48¢ + 24¢   71¢ + 34¢

67¢ + 19¢

29¢ + 33¢   95¢ + 87¢ + 21¢

Sharing Dog Treats

Work in a group.

Act out each problem.

1. 6 dogs share 42 treats fairly.
How many treats does each dog get?
Are there any leftovers?
What is the remainder?

2. 41 treats are shared fairly by 5 dogs.

How many treats does
each dog get?
Are there any leftovers?
What is the remainder?

Peggy made up this problem.
How can you share 27 treats
fairly among 4 dogs?
She drew this picture.

The division sentence for Peggy's problem is:

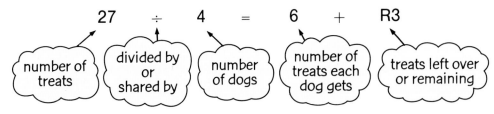

27 ÷ 4 = 6 + R3

| number of treats | divided by or shared by | number of dogs | number of treats each dog gets | treats left over or remaining |

Make up a dog treat problem for each division sentence. Then act it out.

3. 36 shared fairly among 6 is ?

4. 35 shared by 6 = ?

5. 32 divided fairly among 9 equals ?

6. 32 divided by 8 = ?

7. 45 ÷ 7 = ?

8. ? ÷ ? = ?

10

9. Act out sharing the treats between 2 dogs. Record your results in a chart like this. What patterns do you notice?

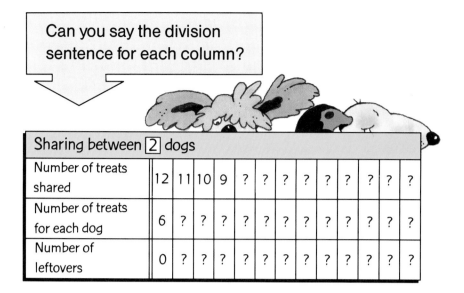

Can you say the division sentence for each column?

Sharing between ⬚2⬚ dogs													
Number of treats shared	12	11	10	9	?	?	?	?	?	?	?	?	?
Number of treats for each dog	6	?	?	?	?	?	?	?	?	?	?	?	?
Number of leftovers	0	?	?	?	?	?	?	?	?	?	?	?	?

10. Continue the pattern from 12 to 24 treats. Use your chart to solve these problems. Then make up 2 problems of your own.

- 2 dogs eat ⬚8⬚ treats each. How many treats are eaten?

- 2 dogs eat ⬚9⬚ treats each with 1 left over. How many treats are shared?

11. Tell what is wrong and why.

There will be 2 treats left over when 2 dogs share 26 treats.

When 2 dogs share 59 treats, there will be 3 treats left over.

12. Use charts like the one for 2 dogs to show sharing with 3 dogs and sharing with 4 dogs.

Tell three things you notice about the charts for sharing with 2 dogs, 3 dogs, and 4 dogs.

Twelve pennies are placed in a row.
Every second coin is replaced by a nickel.
Every third coin is then replaced by a
dime and every fourth coin by a quarter.
What is the value of the coins in the row?

Splitting the Wealth

Class 4A and Class 4B decide to
split the money they raise each day
from selling school banners.

We could put the $1
coins together, then
share them 1 at time.

HILLSIDE SCHOOL

$1.00 each

I've got a simpler idea.

Show how to split this money between
the two classes after the first day.
What division sentence can be used?

Work with a partner.

Act out the problems.
Then write the division sentences.

1. How much will each class have after
   splitting these amounts?

	Day					
	2nd	3rd	4th	5th	6th	7th
Class 4A	8	13	5	10	3	6
Class 4B	10	11	9	10	2	3
Their split	?	?	?	?	?	?

2. Look for a pattern in each chart.

Class 5A	5	6	7	?	?	?
Class 5B	1	2	3	?	?	?
Their split	?	?	?	?	?	?

Class 6A	1	2	3	?	?	?
Class 6B	?	?	?	?	?	?
Their split	4	5	6	?	?	?

Can each amount be split equally?
Why or why not?

3.

4.

After sharing, each person has 3 $1 coins.
How many coins might each person have started with?

5.

6.

How would you split each amount fairly?

7. Marc has a $10 bill. Bonnie has a $20 bill.

8. Katja has a $10 bill. Andrew has a $5 bill.

9. Simone has a quarter. Danny has a $1 coin.

10. Hassan has a $5 bill. Shauna and Megan each have no money.

Take Your Pick

SHARING COUNTERS

There are 24 counters to share. How many people can share them equally with 0 left over?

2 PENNIES LEFT OVER

Bill, Arlene, and Lana share some pennies. Each receives 10 cents, with 2 pennies left over. How many pennies did they start with?

SHARING DOLLARS

Would you rather share some money fairly
with 2 people
OR
with 3 people?
Why?

PLASTICINE PUZZLE

How can 3 children share 7 different-sized pieces of Plasticine fairly?

NONE REMAINING

Place a number in the box so that the result has no remainder.

$$\boxed{?} \div 5 =$$

Find three other numbers that work.

Make up other problems. Post them on the bulletin board for your classmates to solve.

How can you answer these in your head?

3×21

$300 - 80$

$35 + 45$

$78 - 46$

$2 \times \$1.99$

$200 + 8$ $\quad$ $\$3.75 + \$0.99$

$438 - 238$

Identifying Space Creatures

Forming Equal Groups

What name would you give to a ped with 1 leg? 9 legs?

Imagine these kinds of space creatures, called peds.
* They fly in flocks–usually all the same kind.
* They only use their legs for landing, not walking.

    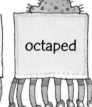

biped $\quad$ triped $\quad$ quadriped $\quad$ pentaped $\quad$ hexaped $\quad$ septaped $\quad$ octaped

Suppose you discovered 21 footprints in the sand.
How many peds could have been there?

Clare drew this diagram.

```
• • •      • • •      • • •      • • •

• • •      • • •      • • •
```

Antonio drew this diagram.

```
• • • • • • •          • • • • • • •

          • • • • • • •
```

You can write:

21 ⟦tri⟧ped legs makes 7 tripeds.

$21 \div ⟦3⟧ = 7$

21 ⟦septa⟧ped legs makes 3 septapeds.

$21 \div ⟦7⟧ = 3$

Model the problems. Then write the division sentences.

1. There were 81 footprints. How many peds could have been there?

2. A flock of octapeds has 56 legs. How many octapeds are there?

3. A flock of peds has 49 legs. How many peds are there?

4. There were 25 footprints. All the creatures were quadripeds except 1. How many quadripeds were there?

5. Create a ped problem of your own.

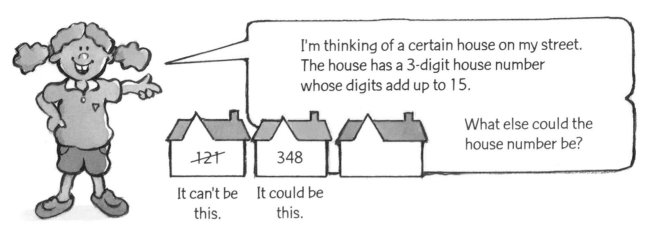

I'm thinking of a certain house on my street. The house has a 3-digit house number whose digits add up to 15.

What else could the house number be?

~~121~~
It can't be this.

348
It could be this.

Making Patios

Try this problem before going on.

PUZZLING PATIO

72 square patio stones are placed in rows of 8.
How many rows are there?

Richard shaded squares on grid paper to help him solve the problem.

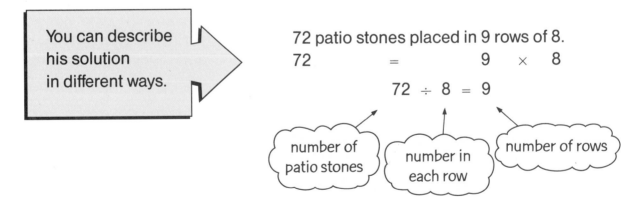

You can describe his solution in different ways.

72 patio stones placed in 9 rows of 8.
72 $=$ 9 $\times$ 8

72 ÷ 8 = 9

number of patio stones

number in each row

number of rows

Work with a partner.

Use squares or grid paper to solve each problem. Then write the division sentence.

1. 42 tiles make ? rows of 6.

2. 38 tiles divided into rows of 5 make ? rows.

3. 38 tiles are placed with
4 in each row.
How many rows are there?

4. 5 tiles are in each row and
there are 26 tiles in all.
How many rows are there?

5. 8 tiles make up a full row.
There are 42 tiles altogether.
How many rows can be made?

6. 3 rows of 9 tiles are laid down
with 2 left over.
How many tiles are there?

Show ONLY the patios that are rectangles.

7. Use 12 patio stones.

8. Use 11 patio stones.

How many patios did you find?
Write a division sentence for each patio you made.

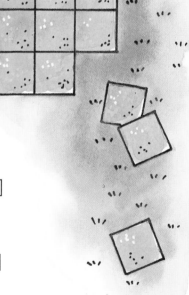

9. Use grid paper to answer the first four questions.

$4 \div 2 = \boxed{?}$ $9 \div 3 = \boxed{?}$ $16 \div 4 = \boxed{?}$ $25 \div 5 = \boxed{?}$

Then look for a pattern to complete the rest.

$36 \div 6 = \boxed{?}$ $49 \div 7 = \boxed{?}$ $64 \div 8 = \boxed{?}$ $81 \div 9 = \boxed{?}$

What shape would the patios be if you made them?

10. If you have 16 squares, how many arrays can you make?
Find numbers that give more arrays.
Find numbers that give only 2 arrays.

TRIANGLES

Trina had lots of marshmallows but only 17 toothpicks to make triangles like this. How many triangles could she make?

CUBES

It takes 6 squares to build 1 cube. Wes used between 30 and 40 squares to build cubes like this. How many cubes did he make?

BASEBALL TEAMS

There are 45 players in a baseball tournament. The same number of players are on each team. How many baseball teams could be in the tournament?

FOUR REMAINING

Place a number in the box so the result has a remainder of 4.

$$\boxed{?} \div 5 = \boxed{?} + R4$$

Find three other numbers that work.

JODIE'S COUNTERS

Jodie placed some counters in groups of 4, and 2 were left over. How many counters could she have started with?

Make up other problems. Post them on the bulletin board for your classmates to solve.

When you press $\boxed{0}$ $\boxed{+}$ $\boxed{2}$ $\boxed{=}$ $\boxed{=}$ $\boxed{=}$ $\boxed{=}$ $\boxed{=}$ $\boxed{=}$ $\boxed{=}$, what happens?

How can you use a calculator to count
by 3s?   by 7s?   by 9s?

Picking Teams

Here are two different ways
to make 4 teams of 7 students
in a class of 28.

Act out each method.

METHOD 1	METHOD 2
28 students form groups of 7.	4 team captains take turns choosing 1 student.

You can write

| 28 divided into 7s = 4 teams | 28 divided among 4 = 7 |
| 28 ÷ 7 = 4 | 28 ÷ 4 = 7 |

Which method uses sharing? grouping?
How are the division sentences related?

Model the situations.
Write the division sentences.

1. activity groups of 3
   27 students in the class

2. 48 students in the gym
   6 relay teams

3. 9 players per volleyball team
   54 volleyball players

4. 35 problem-solvers
   5 teams

Write the related division sentences. Create problems for them.

5. $40 \div 8 = \boxed{?}$

6. $72 \div 9 = \boxed{?}$

7. How many divisions can you find that have only one sentence?

Use your head. Which of these are close to 100?

$$14 + 38 \quad 152 - 47 \quad 75 + 82$$

$$23 \times 4 \quad 64 + 54 \quad 811 - 618 \quad 44 + 64$$

Sharing the Catch

Relating Division to Fractions

12 fish are caught today.
Philip Matoush's share is one third of the catch.

How many fish are in Philip's share?

How did Cecilia use counters on a circle to solve the problem?

You can describe her solution in different ways.

One third of 12 = 4

$\frac{1}{3}$ of 12 = 4

$12 \div 3 = 4$

A Tradition of Sharing

Philip Matoush grins as he pulls a flapping fish from his net. "It's a good year," he says. "White-fish, pike, lake trout—we're catching them all."

Philip is a member of the Cree of Lake Mistassini, 550 km north of Montreal. The Cree pool their catch and share it. If you ask Philip if he'd rather keep all his catch for himself, he just shrugs. "What use would that be?" he asks. "I might have too many fish and someone else might not have enough. The Cree way is to share. It's the best way."

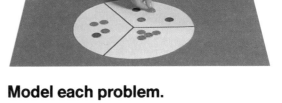

Model each problem.
Write your solution in different ways.

1. How many fish did Philip Matoush get yesterday if the catch was 10 fish?

2. How many fish will Philip get tomorrow if the catch is ? fish?

3. The catch today is 16 fish.
Edward Rabbitskin gets one half.
How many fish does Edward get?

4. Edward's share is $\frac{1}{2}$ of the catch.
☐ fish were caught last week.
How many fish did he get?

5. Yesterday Edward received
7 and $\frac{1}{2}$ fish.
How many fish were caught yesterday?

6. 24 fish are caught today.
Annie Mackinaw gets one fourth.
How many fish does Annie get?

7. The catch yesterday was ☐ fish.
Annie's share is $\frac{1}{4}$.
How many fish did she get?

8. Clarence Wapachee received 3 fish.
The total catch that day was 15 fish.
What fraction was his share?

Make up and solve a sharing problem for each situation below.

9.
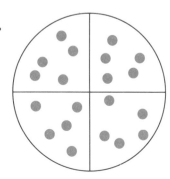

☐ ÷ ☐ = ☐

10.
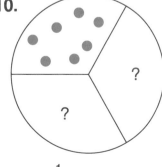

$\frac{1}{3}$ of ☐ = 7

11.
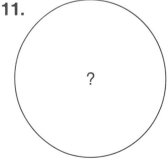

$\frac{1}{☐}$ of 11 = ☐

21

Dividing

There are lots of ways to calculate $22 \div 4$.
Here are some. Can you think of any more?

1. You can count how many groups of 4 are in 22.

(XXXX) (XXXX) (XXXX) (XXXX) (XXXX)   X X

$$22 \div 4 = 5 + R2$$

2. You might use a multiplication table.

$4 \times 5 = 20$ ← 5 is too little

$4 \times 6 = 24$ ← 6 is too much

X	1	2	3	4	5	6
1	1	2	3	4	5	6
2	2	4	6	8	10	12
3	3	6	9	12	15	18
4	4	8	12	16	(20)	24
5	5	10	15	20	25	30
6	6	12	18	24	30	36

$20 \div 4 = 5$

20 is 2 less than 22,

so

$22 \div 4 = 5 + R2$.

3. You might see how many times to subtract
groups of 4 from 22 before you have less than 4 left.

22 ($- 4 - 4 - 4 - 4 - 4$)   Subtract five 4s to get 2 left. $22 \div 4 = 5 + R2$

4. You might see how many times to add
groups of 4 to get close to 22.

($4 + 4 + 4 + 4 + 4$)   Add five 4s to get 20.
Then add 2 to get 22.

$22 \div 4 = 5 + R2$

Work in a group.

Show two different ways
to do each division.

1. $32 \div 5$ **2.** $27 \div 7$

3. $56 \div 8$ **4.** $56 \div 9$

5. $56 \div 10$ **6.** $24 \div 2$

HOW MANY COUNTERS?

Divide a bag of counters into ? equal piles. How many counters might be left over?

CIRCLE MAT

Find $\frac{1}{2}$ of 24,

$\frac{1}{4}$ of 24,

$\frac{1}{6}$ of 24,

and $\frac{1}{8}$ of 24.

BIG NUMBERS

Manoli has 65 pictures to post on 3 bulletin boards.

Finish his work.
Use his idea to divide 72 by 4.

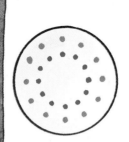

I need to figure $65 \div 3$. But 10 on each board is 30. So $65 - 30$ is 35 left to divide.

HOW ARE THEY ALIKE?

Solve, using counters if you need to. How are the answers alike?

$$5 \div 5 = \boxed{?} \qquad 5 \div 1 = \boxed{?}$$
$$8 \div 8 = \boxed{?} \qquad 8 \div 1 = \boxed{?}$$
$$12 \div 12 = \boxed{?} \qquad 12 \div 1 = \boxed{?}$$
$$100 \div 100 = \boxed{?} \qquad 100 \div 1 = \boxed{?}$$
$$\boxed{?} \div \boxed{?} = \boxed{?} \qquad \boxed{?} \div \boxed{?} = \boxed{?}$$

WHICH IS LARGER?

Which division gives the larger result? Why?

$\$ 12 \div 3$ or $\$ 12 \div 5$?
$\$100 \div 7$ or $\$100 \div 12$?
$\$ 14 \div 4$ or $\$ 19 \div 4$?
$\$100 \div 4$ or $\$200 \div 4$?

Make up other problems. Post them on the bulletin board for your classmates to solve.

Solving a Problem by Making a List

Try this problem before going on.

THE SUM IS 8

Pick any two-digit number, like 62 or 35, where the sum of the digits is 8.
Divide the number by 9.
What is the remainder?

Jeremy's class solved the problem by making an organized list.

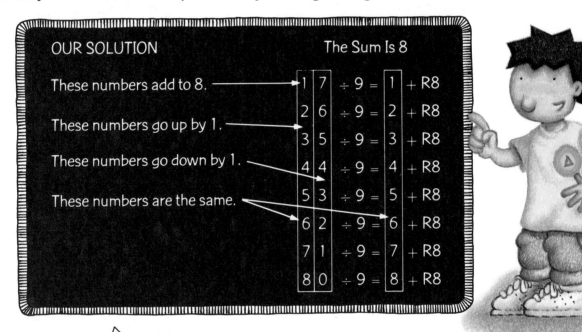

OUR SOLUTION   The Sum Is 8

These numbers add to 8. ———→ | 1 | 7 | ÷ 9 = | 1 | + R8

These numbers go up by 1. ——→ | 2 | 6 | ÷ 9 = | 2 | + R8

                                | 3 | 5 | ÷ 9 = | 3 | + R8

These numbers go down by 1. → | 4 | 4 | ÷ 9 = | 4 | + R8

                                | 5 | 3 | ÷ 9 = | 5 | + R8

These numbers are the same. → | 6 | 2 | ÷ 9 = | 6 | + R8

                                | 7 | 1 | ÷ 9 = | 7 | + R8

                                | 8 | 0 | ÷ 9 = | 8 | + R8

Work in a group. **Solve these problems by making an organized list.**

GROUPS OF 9

Start with numbers less than 100.
Find which ones give no remainder when you form groups of 9.
How many numbers do this?
How do you know?

SHAHIN'S COUNTERS

Shahin placed some counters in groups of 4, and 3 were left over. Then he placed the same number of counters in groups of 5, and 2 were left over. How many counters could he have had to start with?

MYSTERY MONEY

I am holding 2 coins in one hand. What different amounts of money could be in my hand?

Write a problem for each of these. Then solve.

1. 36 ÷ 6 **2.** 21 ÷ 7 **3.** $\frac{1}{2}$ of 13 **4.** one-third of 27

Solve ONLY the problems where you could use division.

5. Lee places 54 stickers equally among 6 pages. How many stickers are on each page?

6. The cook made 28 pancakes for the 7 campers. Each camper got the same number. How many pancakes did each get?

7. Travis has 28 seeds. He plants 5 in each pot. How many pots does he need?

8. Narinder gave Adelle one third of her 24 raffle tickets to sell. How many tickets did Adelle receive?

9. Ken grows pumpkins to sell. He sold 21 of them. Then he had 7 left. How many did he grow?

10. Chris uses 2 shelves to hold 16 books. Each shelf holds the same number of books. How many are on each shelf?

11. Jean made 16 space creatures with 4 legs each. How many legs are there?

12. How many buns are in one half dozen? How many are in one quarter dozen?

Playing Games for Practice

Play each game in a group of 2, 3, or 4.

Remainders

- Roll one die twice to create a two-digit number.
- Roll the die again to get a number to divide by.
- Do the division.
- The remainder is the number of spaces that you move on the gameboard.

Example

▞ then ⠇⠇ Start number is 34.

⠇⠇ Divide by 6.

$34 \div 6 = 5 + R4$

Move 4 spaces.

Fifty Fill-Up

- Shuffle the cards. Place them face down in a pile.
- Turn over the top card.
- Find a number on your own fifties chart that matches the card.
- Place a counter on that number. (Only 1 counter is allowed on a square.)
- Place the card face down under the pile.
- Take turns until no more counters can be placed.
- The winner is the player with the greatest number of counters on his or her chart.

A multiple of 2	Shared by 2 with 0 left over	Not a multiple of 2	Shared by 3 with 1 left over	A multiple of 3	Shared by 3 with 2 left over
A multiple of 5	A multiple of 7	A multiple of 4	Shared by 4 with 2 left over	A multiple of 11	A multiple of 13

Variation: The winner is the first player to get 3 counters in a row.

EXPLAIN THIS!

Why can't $12 \div 3$ and $3 \div 12$ have the same answer? Write your explanation.

LOOK FOR A RULE

What is the largest remainder you can have when you divide a number by 4? by 7? by 31?

BLAST FROM THE PAST

These problems might have been in your grandparents' math books. How would you solve them?

1. What is one third of a dozen eggs?
2. Mary has 21 chicks. John has one third as many chicks as Mary. How many does John have?

BRAIN POWER

If $6 \div 2 = 3$,

then

$60 \div 2 = \boxed{?}$

$600 \div 2 = \boxed{?}$

PLAYGROUND WHEELS

The total number of bicycles and tricycles at the playground is 7. I count 16 wheels in all. How many tricycles are there? How many bicycles?

Make up other problems. Post them on the bulletin board for your classmates to solve.

1. Forty children sign up for floor hockey. There are 5 teams. How many children are on each team?

2. 12 fish are caught. Alfred Coomish gets one third of the catch. How many fish are left for the others?

3. Sherry and Aaron played table tennis. Sherry won with a score of 15. She won by 5 points. What was Aaron's score?

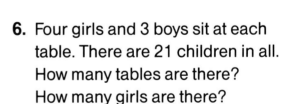

4. Geoff, Blair, Kasia, and Denise share 38 hockey cards equally. How many cards are left over?

5. What number of counters can you share equally among 4 people? Can this number also be shared among 3 without a remainder?

6. Four girls and 3 boys sit at each table. There are 21 children in all. How many tables are there? How many girls are there?

7. Luisa has 18 balloons. How many more balloons does she need to make 6 bunches of 4 balloons?

8. Show three different ways to solve $37 \div 4$.

9. Write a problem for $20 \div 4$ and solve it.

10. Write three division sentences that have the answer 8.

Write to someone younger, telling how to find

18 ÷ 4

What is your favorite number to divide by?
Write a note to a friend telling why.

Knowing how to multiply helps you to divide. Tell how.

Tell why Amos has not finished dividing 24 by 4.

I found 5 groups of 4 and 4 remainder.

What questions do you still have about division?

6 × 5 = 30

Tell how this fact helps you find

36 ÷ 5

Exploring

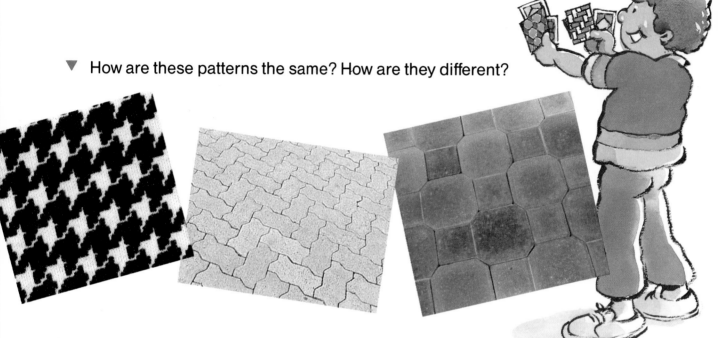

▼ How are these patterns the same? How are they different?

▲
Are there any gaps in this floor pattern?

Are there any places where the shapes overlap?

▲
How many different shapes are used in this quilt pattern?

Model it using pattern blocks.

Tiling Patterns

Artists made these 3 patterns for fabrics and wrapping paper.
Describe the shapes in each pattern.

Trace one of the shapes. ▶

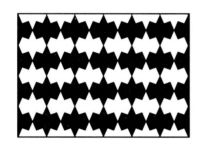

▼ This is a honeycomb. Why do you think we can call it a tiling pattern?

▶ This is a geodesic dome. What is the basic shape the architect used?

Tell where you have seen patterns with shapes in your home or neighborhood.

The numbers on the T-shirts form a pattern.
Which number belongs on the last shirt?

Making Counter Top Designs

Use pattern blocks.

1. Jessica chose the hexagon and modelled the counter top.
   Are there other tiling patterns she could make with the hexagons?

2. Choose another pattern block shape. Make a counter top using that shape. Tell why you chose your shape.

3. Cleo chose the triangle. Model what her counter top looks like.
   Are there other tiling patterns she could make with the triangles?

4. Jessica found another shape in Cleo's triangle pattern. Which shape do you think she saw?

5. Make a tiling pattern using a different pattern block shape. Describe any other shapes you see in your pattern.

6. Use dot paper to record the tiling pattern you made. Use color to show the pattern. Ask your partner to describe your design.

7. Tell your partner how to make this pattern with blocks. Try using the words *flip, slide,* or *turn.*

I see flips and slides here.

I see turns and flips.

8. Draw another tiling pattern on dot paper. Use the words *slide, flip,* or *turn* to help your partner make the pattern with blocks.

9. How can you use color to show slides in a tiling pattern? How can you show flips?

10. Design a tiling pattern using one pattern block shape. Write a set of instructions for making the pattern. Give the instructions to another pair to follow. Do they draw the pattern correctly? If not, find out why.

33

How can you do these in your head?

$$470 - 350$$

$$\begin{array}{r} \$48 \\ - 29 \\ \hline \end{array}$$

$$6 \times 5 \times 2$$

$$25 + 66$$

$$50 + 40 + 8$$

$$25 + 35$$

$$\$33 + \$59$$

Stacking Shapes

How does the square tiling pattern help explain why the cubes fill space with no gaps?

Work in a group.

1. Make a model of a prism using square pattern blocks.
   How would you describe the prism?
   Show that the prism makes a tiling pattern.

2. Choose a different pattern block.
   Make a model of a prism using the blocks.
   How would you describe the prism?
   Show that the prism makes a tiling pattern.

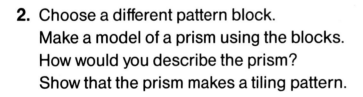

3. Do you think prisms with each of these bases will make tiling patterns? Why or why not?

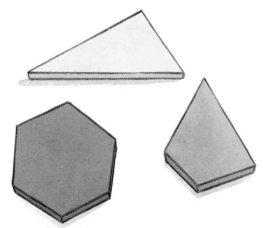

4. Can any of these geometric shapes be used to make tiling patterns?

DOES IT WORK?

Can you make a tiling pattern using one of these pentagons?

ELASTIC SQUARES

How many of Carla's squares can you fit on the geoboard without overlapping?

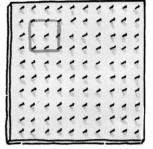

MIRROR! MIRROR!

Make a triangle that has 1 square corner. What different shapes can you make if you place a mirror along 1 edge?

JACKET DESIGN

Tell how the border on this jacket can be made using 1 triangle. Use the words **slide, flip,** or **turn.**

TOWER BUILDING

How many more blocks does Jethro need? He wants to make a tower like this, but 5 levels high.

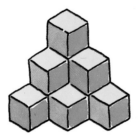

Make up other problems. Post them on the bulletin board for your classmates to solve.

Which numbers have a total between 300 and 500?

394

Find two numbers with a difference of about 100.

612

483

135

88

571

Which numbers add up to about 800?

240

Combining Squares

The game of Dominoes has pieces made of 2 squares that share a side.

1. Are these dominoes the same shape or different? How can you tell?

How many different shapes of dominoes are there?

Pretend you have a game called Triominoes.
The pieces are made of 3 squares that share at least 1 full side.

2. These are not triominoes. Why?

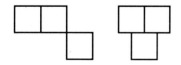

3. Are these triominoes the same shape or different? Why do you think so?

4. Use square blocks to model the triominoes. Then cut each shape out of grid paper. How many different shapes can you make?

5. Cut out 10 copies of one triomino and make a tiling pattern. Describe the pattern using the words *slide*, *flip*, or *turn*.

Use square blocks and grid paper.

Tetrominoes use 4 squares that share at least 1 full side.

6. How many different tetrominoes can you make?

> I can flip or turn this shape to match the others. These shapes are the same.

7. Cut out 10 copies of each tetromino and make a tiling pattern.
Describe each pattern using the words *slide, flip,* or *turn.*
Which pattern was the easiest to do?
Why?

8. All the triominoes have line symmetry.

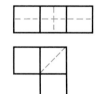

The fold line is a line of symmetry. It divides the shape into matching halves.

Do all the tetrominoes have line symmetry?

9. What do you think a pentomino is?
Model, then cut out, as many different pentominoes as you can.

10. Choose one pentomino and make a tiling pattern. Describe it.
Are any patterns in your group alike? How?

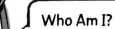
Who Am I?

1. I am an odd number.
   My tens digit is odd.
   My ones digit is less than 6.
   The difference of my digits is 8.

2. I am greater than 30.
   I am less than 50.
   One of my factors is 5.
   The product of my digits is 15.

Combining Pattern Blocks

Work with a partner.

1. Use 2 different pattern blocks
   to make a tiling pattern.
   Trace around the blocks to record
   your pattern on paper.
   Try to make a different pattern
   using the same blocks. Record it.

2. On your paper pattern, outline 2
   joining shapes to show a new,
   bigger shape.
   Name your new shape.
   Outline every example of this
   shape in your pattern. Make
   sure there are no gaps.

3. Use 3 different pattern blocks to
   make a tiling pattern.
   Trace around the blocks to
   record your pattern on paper.
   Try to make a different pattern
   using the same blocks. Record it.

4. On your paper pattern, color 2
   or 3 joining shapes to show a
   new, bigger shape.
   Name your new shape.
   Color the tiling pattern made
   with these shapes.

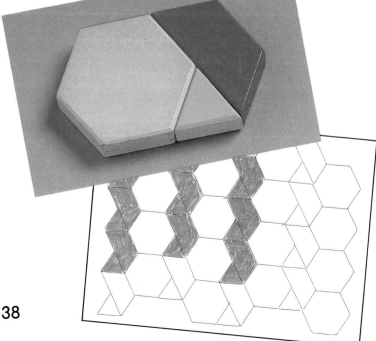

BROKEN SQUARES

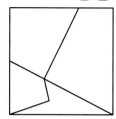

Cut 4 identical squares like this. Try to make a tiling pattern with all the pieces.

ARROWHEADS

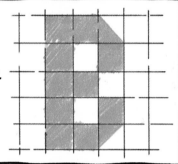

Use this shape to make a tiling pattern.
Record your design.
Do other arrowheads make tiling patterns?

SYMMETRIC LETTERS

Shade squares on grid paper to make a capital letter.
Is the letter symmetric? Explain.
Make a tiling pattern with it if you can.
Try different letters.

COOKIE CUTTERS

How can you cut the cookie dough so there are no gaps between the cookies?

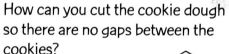
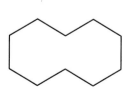
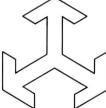
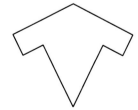

TOOLHPICKS AND HEXAGONS

Bruno is making a row of hexagons with toothpicks.
How many toothpicks does he need for 12 hexagons?

Make up other problems. Post them on the bulletin board for your classmates to solve.

Solving a Problem by Using a Pattern

Try this problem before going on.

A TRIANGLE TILE

How many toothpicks and how many marshmallows do you need to make a row of 8 triangles?

Toshi's group extended the problem to 20 triangles. They looked for a pattern to solve it.

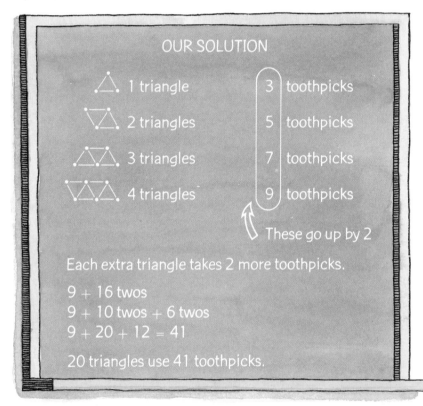

OUR SOLUTION

△ 1 triangle	3	toothpicks
▽ 2 triangles	5	toothpicks
△△ 3 triangles	7	toothpicks
▽△ 4 triangles	9	toothpicks

These go up by 2

Each extra triangle takes 2 more toothpicks.

9 + 16 twos
9 + 10 twos + 6 twos
9 + 20 + 12 = 41

20 triangles use 41 toothpicks.

Finish the group's solution to find the number of marshmallows needed.

Work in a group.

Solve these problems by using a pattern.

MARSHMALLOW SQUARES

How many toothpicks and marshmallows do you need for a tiling pattern of 20 squares?

STEPPING UP

This staircase uses 6 blocks for 3 steps. How many blocks do you need to make 10 steps?

HALF AND HALF

A large piece of paper is cut in half. Each half is cut in half. Again, each half is cut in half. How many pieces are there after 5 cuts?

1. Tell if each of these shapes can be used to make a tiling pattern. Why do you think so?

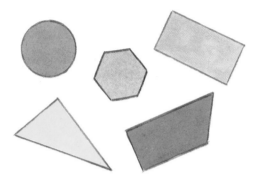

2. Trace this parallelogram. Use it to make a tiling pattern.

3. Draw a tetromino that looks like

if you flip it.

4. Start with any triangle. Describe how to make a tiling pattern using the words *slide*, *flip*, or *turn*.

5. Elliott is putting 12 designs on the bulletin board. How many tacks does he need?

6. Use this net to make a pyramid.

How many faces does the pyramid have? How many edges? corners?

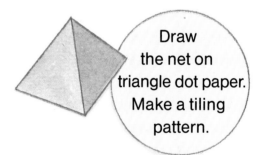

Draw the net on triangle dot paper. Make a tiling pattern.

7. Trace and cut out 2 different pattern block shapes. Can you fold each shape so that one half matches the other? Draw the lines of symmetry on the shapes.

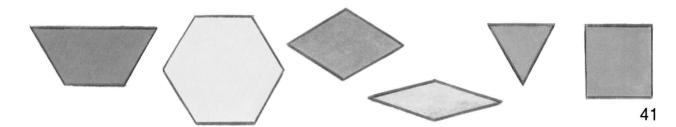

Play each game in a group of 2, 3, or 4.

Pentomino Puzzle

- Share the pentominoes equally.
- In turn, each player puts a pentomino on the gameboard. (No overlapping of squares.)
- The last player able to place a pentomino on the board is the winner.

Example

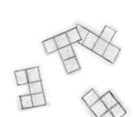

Variations: • The winner is the player who places the most pieces in 3 games.
- The last player gets 1 point. The winner is the first one with 3 points.

Tricky Triangles

- Cut out a triangle from stiff paper. Use it to make the tracings.
- The first player traces around the triangle on a plain piece of paper.
- In turn, each player traces the triangle so that one side matches a side of a triangle already on the paper.
- The last player to trace a triangle without going off the paper is the winner.

Example

Variation: Use a quadrilateral (4-sided shape) instead of a triangle.

THE X SQUARE

Cut a square like this.
Use the 4 triangles to
make a new shape.
What tiling pattern can you
make using the new shape?

TETRAHEXES

Tetrahexes are made with 4 hexagons. How
many different tetrahexes can you make?

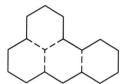

Use one to make a tiling pattern.

COLORED WINDOWS

Jahi is fitting colored glass into
this window. He has red panes
and blue panes.
How many different designs can
he make?

STACKING CANS

A display like this in a grocery
store is 10 cans high.
How many cans are there
altogether?

WINDMILLS

Use this tile to make a tiling
pattern.

**Make up other problems. Post
them on the bulletin board for
your classmates to solve.**

1. Use the square and trapezoid pattern blocks to make a tiling pattern. Record your pattern.

2. Why do you think tiles are not usually in the shape of a circle?

3. Design a tile to use with a circle to make a tiling pattern. Record your pattern.

4. Draw the new shape when you flip a triangle.
    Tell how the flip line is like a line of symmetry.

— flip line

5. Draw a shape that will not make a tiling pattern by itself. Show why.

6. When 2 square tables are pushed together, 6 people can be seated.
    18 people are coming to dinner.
    How many square tables are needed for one long table?

7. Show how to put 3 identical triangles together to form a row.

8. Pick a shape that you know will make a tiling pattern. Put 2 of these shapes together to form a new tile. Try to make a tiling pattern with this new tile. Explain why you can or why you cannot.

This shape tiles.

This shape does not tile.

Tell why.

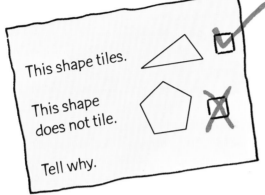

Why do you think most real-world tiles are squares?

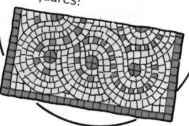

Describe the most interesting tiling pattern you found outside of school to a friend.
Make a sketch of the pattern.

Find a tiling pattern you like on the bulletin board. Pretend to phone your partner. Describe the pattern so your partner can build it.

Write to a friend. Explain what a tiling pattern is and where some examples might be found.

What questions do you still have about tiling patterns?

Exploring Fractions

How many triangles can 12 students form?

What fraction of all the triangles is 1 triangle?

What fraction of all the students are in 1 triangle?

How many hexagons can 12 students form? ▶

What fraction of all the hexagons is 1 hexagon?

What fraction of all the students are in 1 hexagon?

How many squares can 12 students form?

What fraction of all the squares is 1 square?

What fraction of all the students are in 1 square?

and Decimals

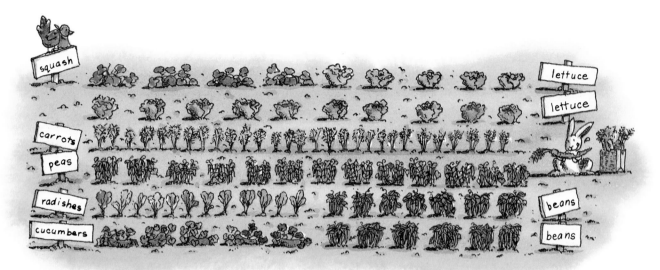

▲ Which vegetables take up about one and a half rows?

Which vegetables take up less than $1\frac{1}{2}$ rows?

Draw what the garden might look like if $2\frac{1}{2}$ rows were planted with lettuce and the rest with beans and cucumbers?

◀ What time will it be in $\frac{1}{4}$ of an hour?

Use a fraction to tell how long it is from 9:45 until recess time.

How long does recess last?

Tell how long it is from the end of recess until lunch.

Write about two ways you or someone in your family uses fractions.

Do you ever use decimals? When?

47

Use your head. Watch the signs.

3×9	$28 - 7$	$9 + 8$
9×3	$18 + 9$	$56 + 8$
8×6	8×7	8×9
9×8	$9 + 56$	$34 - 6$

Coloring Flags

Naming Fractions as Parts of a Whole

The **numerator** of a fraction tells you how many equal parts to count.

The **denominator** tells you how many equal parts there are altogether.

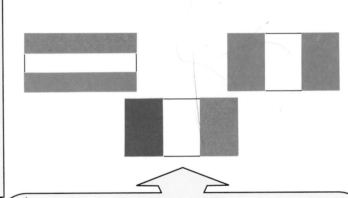

$\frac{1}{3}$ of each flag is white.

Use thirds to describe each flag another way.

Work with a partner.

1. Which flags show $\frac{1}{3}$? Which show $\frac{2}{3}$? Which do not show thirds? Why?

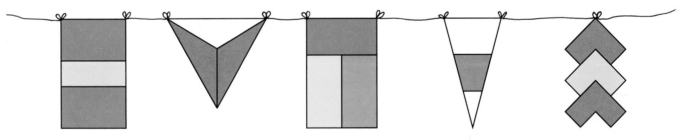

2. Make different flags with 4 equal parts, using 2 colors.
What fractions can you show?

3. Make different flags with 6 equal parts, using 2 or 3 colors.
What fractions can you show?

48

About how many?

21 newspapers a day for a week

8 hours sleep a night for April

$2.25 an hour for 6 hours

22 cars per parking lot for 5 parking lots

Finding Sticker-Strip Fractions

Naming Fractions as Parts of a Group

Act out each problem using a strip of 12 stickers.

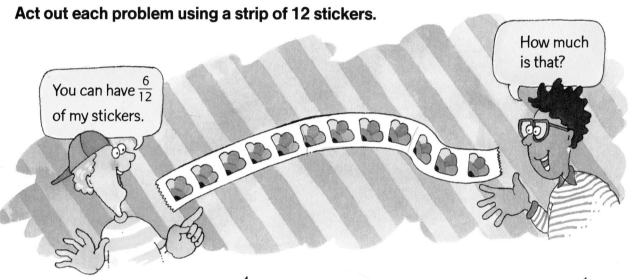

You can have $\frac{6}{12}$ of my stickers.

How much is that?

1. How many stickers are on a $\frac{4}{12}$ strip? a $\frac{1}{3}$ strip? a $\frac{2}{3}$ strip?

2. If you have a whole strip and a $\frac{1}{4}$ strip, how many stickers do you have? Explain.

3. Make up a problem about whole strips and part strips for a friend to solve.

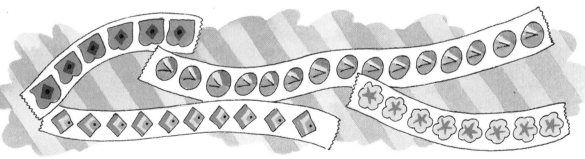

Work with a partner.

Use strips with different numbers of stickers.

4. Do you think it is easier to show $\frac{1}{5}$ of 12 stickers or $\frac{1}{5}$ of 20 stickers? Why?

5. How many stickers might be on a strip if it is easy to show $\frac{1}{3}$?

49

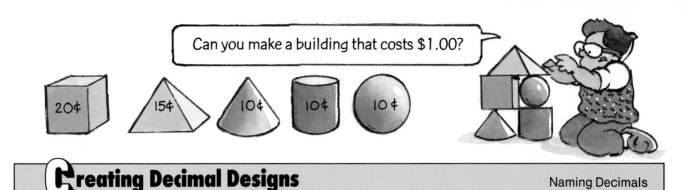

Can you make a building that costs $1.00?

20¢   15¢   10¢   10¢   10¢

Creating Decimal Designs

Each of these whole squares is divided into smaller parts.

4 equal parts means you have fourths.

9 equal parts means you have ninths.

100 equal parts means you have hundredths.

You can write the name for each part using a fraction or a decimal, 1 hundredth or $\frac{1}{100}$ or 0.01.

The white part is 40 hundredths or $\frac{40}{100}$ or 0.40. How much of the whole square is the colored part?

Work with a partner.

1. How much of the whole square does each animal cover? Write your solutions in different ways.

2. How many rows are in each whole square? How much of the square does 1 row cover? do 3 rows cover? Write your solutions as decimals.

Use a hundredths grid.

3. Design 2 creatures of your own. How much of the whole grid do you use each time?

4. Can you design a creature using 0.98 of the grid? more than 1 whole grid?

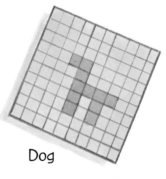

Dog

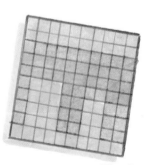

Elephant

Bear's head

REPEATING A PATTERN

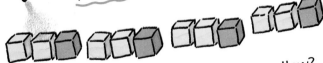

What fraction of the cubes shown are yellow?

If there are 24 cubes, how many are yellow?

COUNT THE TWOS

Luis said that 0.23 of the numbers from 1 to 100 contain the digit 2. Is he correct?

THE RING

What fraction of the whole square is each color?

What fraction of the ring is each color?

SPRING PLANTING

About what fraction of the yard is grass?
Tell why you think so.

3 LARGER SQUARES

A grid has 100 small squares. Color in 3 larger squares so that they cover about 0.5 of the grid altogether. Write the decimals that describe each square you colored.

Make up other problems. Post them on the bulletin board for your classmates to solve.

$$\begin{array}{r} 4\ 9\ \boxed{?} \\ +\ \boxed{?}\ 0\ 4 \\ \hline 7\ \boxed{?}\ 9 \end{array}$$

$$\begin{array}{r} 8\ \boxed{?}\ 8 \\ -\ 3\ 5\ \boxed{?} \\ \hline \boxed{?}\ 4\ 6 \end{array}$$

$$\begin{array}{r} \boxed{?}\ 4\ \boxed{?} \\ +\ 1\ \boxed{?}\ 6 \\ \hline 5\ 6\ \boxed{?} \end{array}$$

$$\begin{array}{r} 3\ \boxed{?}\ \boxed{?} \\ -\ 1\ \boxed{?}\ 3 \\ \hline \boxed{?}\ 8\ 2 \end{array}$$

$$\begin{array}{r} 2\ \boxed{?}\ 1 \\ 3\ 4\ 7 \\ +\ \boxed{?}\ \boxed{?}\ \boxed{?} \\ \hline 8\ 2\ 8 \end{array}$$

Covering the Hexagon

Let's suppose the yellow hexagon is 1 whole.

Work in a group.

Use the yellow, red, blue, and green pattern blocks.

1. What fraction of the whole is the trapezoid? the parallelogram? the triangle?

2. Model each amount.

   $\frac{2}{3}$ $\frac{5}{6}$ $1\frac{2}{3}$

   Now draw your models on triangle dot paper.

3. Use the blocks to show 2 halves. What fraction can you write? What whole number?

4. Use blocks that are all of one color. Find other fraction names for 1. Then find other names for 2, 3, and 4.

5. Is Marlene right? Why or why not?

My right hand has $1\frac{1}{2}$.
My left hand has $\frac{3}{2}$.
Which is more?

I think three halves is more.

6. Cover hexagons using these pieces. Find two names for each covered amount.

- 5 red
- 7 blue
- 6 red
- 8 green
- 6 blue
- 12 green

7. Use yellow pieces and pieces of one other color to show each amount. How many pieces do you need?

$$\frac{8}{3} \qquad \frac{16}{6} \qquad \frac{10}{2}$$

8. Use pieces that are all of one color to find a different name for each amount.

$$2\frac{1}{6} \qquad 3\frac{2}{3} \qquad 4\frac{1}{2}$$

9.

My red and yellow design is named $3\frac{3}{2}$.

If I cover my design with all red pieces, what's its new name?

I can't make that design work with blue pieces. Why not?

I can make the same design using just yellow and green pieces. What's the name of my design?

What if I use only green pieces?

10. Find three different fraction names for each design.

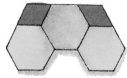

Now use some of your favorite pieces to make a design.
Give it a fraction name. Try to name it another way.

Complete each pattern. ⇨ 52, 65, 78, ?, ?, ?

⤵ 15, 21, 26, 30, ?, ?, ?

Now make up
one of your own. ⬊ A, D, G, ?, ?, ?

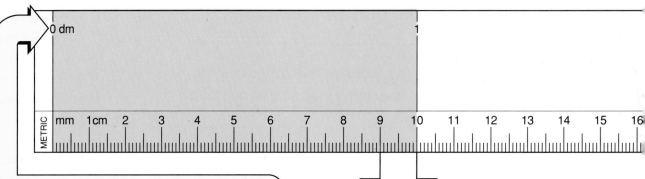

This colored part of a metre stick
shows a distance of 1 decimetre.
How many decimetres are in a metre?
What fraction of a metre is 1 dm?
Write this as a decimal.

How many decimetres are shown in
this picture?
Write the decimal to describe it as
part of a metre.

This shows a distance of 1 centimetre.
How many centimetres are in a metre?
What fraction of a metre is 1 cm?
Write this as a decimal.

How many centimetres are shown in
this picture?
Write the decimal to describe it as
part of a metre.

1. Is Leanne right? Why or why not?

Finish her table.

10 cm	0.10 m	1 dm	0.1 m
20 cm	0.20 m	2 dm	0.2 m
30 cm	?	?	?

One tenth is the same as
ten hundredths. You can
write   0.1 = 0.10

What patterns do you notice?

54

2. Is Jim right?
Why or why not?

Chantel is 112 cm tall.
That's more than a metre
but only a little bit more.
She must be 1.12 m tall.

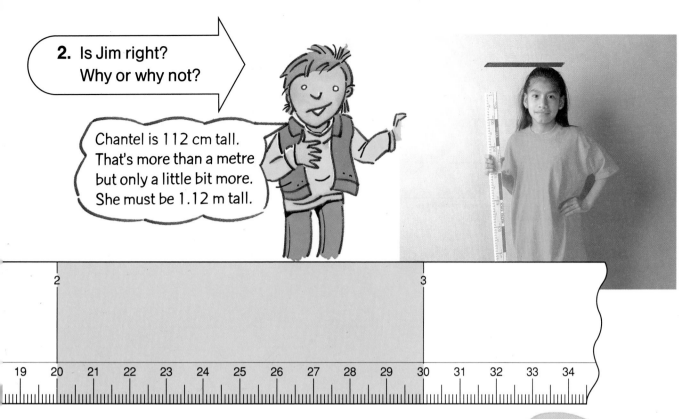

3. How many centimetres are these heights?

0.57 m   2.04 m   5.23 m

Who do you think would be this tall?

4. Use decimals to describe these as metres.

9 cm   146 cm $\boxed{?}$ cm

Estimate each height from the floor.
Then measure to see how close you were.

5. Use decimals to describe these as metres.

11 dm   36 dm $\boxed{?}$ dm

Estimate each distance on the floor.
Then measure to see how close you were.

6. A tree is 3.$\boxed{?}$2 m tall.
What is the greatest height it could be?
the least height?

55

Use different numbers to complete the magic square.

The sums of each column (↕), each row (↔), and each diagonal (↗↘) are the same.

Counting Pennies

How much is half a dollar?

Tell how the grid with pennies shows that $\frac{50}{100} = \frac{1}{2}$.

What decimals can you write for $\frac{50}{100}$? for $\frac{1}{2}$?

Work with a partner.

Use pennies on a grid.

1. Find decimal names for these amounts. Describe any patterns you see. $\frac{1}{4}$ $\frac{2}{4}$ $\frac{3}{4}$ $\frac{4}{4}$

2. Find decimal names for these amounts. Tell how you found them. $\frac{1}{10}$ $\frac{1}{5}$ $1\frac{3}{10}$ $2\frac{2}{5}$ $\frac{1}{20}$

Color a hundredths grid or tenths grid.

3. Is Lauren's work correct? Explain.

4. Write two decimal names for these amounts.
   $\frac{7}{10}$ $1\frac{1}{2}$ $\frac{3}{5}$

5. Write two fraction names for these decimals.
   0.3   2.75   3.6

6. Do you think any fraction names on the hundredths grid use thirds? Explain.

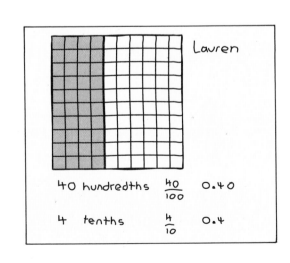

Lauren

40 hundredths $\frac{40}{100}$ 0.40

4 tenths $\frac{4}{10}$ 0.4

56

Take Your Pick

A NUMERATOR OF 2

Find three digits to make this statement true.

0. $\boxed{?}$ $\boxed{?}$ is another name for $\frac{2}{\boxed{?}}$.

SPECIAL AMOUNTS

$$\frac{6}{3} \quad \frac{9}{3} \quad \frac{12}{3} \quad \frac{15}{3}$$

These are special amounts of thirds. Why?

Name 4 special amounts of fourths.

DIFFERENT POINTS OF VIEW

A square is 4 cm by 4 cm.
If the square has a value of 1,
show 0.75 in three different ways.

ANOTHER NAME?

Use dot paper to help you
find another name for $2\frac{2}{3}$.
Is there a name for $2\frac{2}{3}$ using
fourths? Why or why not?

FILL IN THE BLANKS

The five numbers 0.85, 60, 0.60, $\frac{1}{4}$, and $\frac{3}{5}$ belong in the story.
Find a place for each. Explain how you did it.

Celka has $\boxed{?}$ cents, which is $\boxed{?}$ of a
dollar. Another name for that money is
$\boxed{?}$ of a dollar. Celka wants to buy a candy
bar that costs $\boxed{?}$ of a dollar. She borrows
$\boxed{?}$ of a dollar from her brother. Then she
has enough.

**Make up other problems. Post them on the bulletin
board for your classmates to solve.**

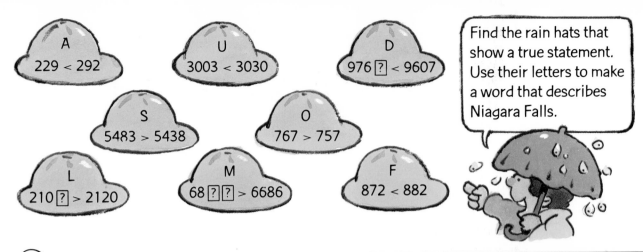

Find the rain hats that show a true statement. Use their letters to make a word that describes Niagara Falls.

A
229 < 292

U
3003 < 3030

D
976 ? < 9607

S
5483 > 5438

O
767 > 757

L
210 ? > 2120

M
68 ? ? > 6686

F
872 < 882

Comparing Decimal Distances

Comparing Decimals

	Lars	John	Richard	Tara
Kleenex Kick	1.05m	1.3 m	1.25m	1.1m
Penny Thumb Toss	1.88m	2.1m	2.12 m	1.86m
Cotton Ball Puff	0.95 m	0.97m	1.3 m	1.34m

1. Who won the kleenex kick? Tell how you know.

2. Who won the other events?

3. Estimate each winning distance on the floor. Then measure to see how close you were.

4. Did anyone puff the cotton ball farther than they kicked the kleenex? If so, who? How much farther?

5. Kris tried the kleenex kick and did better than Richard. He didn't do as well as John. What distance might Kris have kicked the kleenex?

6. Six girls finished the
   penny thumb toss
   in this order.

Aminah	1.98 m
Tara	?
Cleo	?
Jessica	?
Chantel	?
Anya	1.88 m

Find possible distances
for those who finished
second, third, fourth, and
fifth. There were no ties.

7. John wrote the distances from the cotton
   ball puff.

   95 cm   97 cm   1.3 m   1.34 m

   97 is the biggest number. Why didn't that
   distance win?

8. Miguel puffed the cotton ball 1.2 m.
   Susan puffed it $1\frac{1}{2}$ times as far.
   How far did Susan puff it?

Have your own cotton ball puff, penny thumb toss,
or kleenex kick.

9. Estimate whether each distance is greater than or
   less than a metre.
   Then measure it to the nearest hundredth of a metre.
   Put the scores in order.

I scored 99 in this dart game. How many darts did I throw? Where did they hit the target?

Who had more pizza?

Monique shaded fraction circles to help her solve the problem.

I had $1\frac{1}{3}$ minipizzas.

I had $1\frac{1}{2}$ minipizzas.

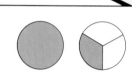

How can you tell that $1\frac{1}{2}$ is more than $1\frac{1}{3}$?

 **Work with a partner.**

Use fraction circles.

1. Kareem ate $\frac{2}{5}$ of a pepperoni pizza and Al ate $\frac{2}{3}$ of a mushroom pizza.

   Each boy ate 2 pieces. Who ate more? How do you know?

2. Larry ate $2\frac{2}{4}$ minipizzas. Franca ate $2\frac{3}{4}$ minipizzas. Can you tell who ate more without using a diagram?

3. $\boxed{\frac{4}{5} \text{ of a pizza}}$ **or** $\boxed{\frac{4}{3} \text{ of a pizza}}$

   Which is less? Find at least 2 ways to show this.

4. Model each pair of fractions. Which is bigger?

   $\boxed{\frac{2}{3}, \frac{3}{4}}$ $\boxed{\frac{3}{4}, \frac{4}{5}}$ $\boxed{\frac{4}{5}, \frac{5}{6}}$

   Find two other pairs like these.

60

Model your solutions.

5. Hana and Diane each ate 4 pieces. Who ate more pizza, Hana or Diane? Tell why you think so.

6. Katelyn and Shalini each ate 5 pieces. Who ate the same amount of pizza as Diane? Tell how you know.

7. Who ate the most pizza? How do you know?

8. How much of Shalini's pizza is the same as 2 pieces of Diane's? 4 pieces of Diane's? 6 pieces of Diane's?

9. Make up your own pizza problems for another pair to solve.

9. Make up your own pizza problems for another pair to solve.

WHERE'S THE MISTAKE?

Five nine-year-olds measured their heights and recorded them like this.

Which measurements are probably wrong?

What do you think the correct measurements might be?

123 m
1.3 m
132 cm
182 cm
1.28 cm

YUMMY PIZZA

A pizza has 10 slices.
0.5 of the pizza has pepperoni.
0.7 of the pizza has mushrooms.
0.3 of the pizza has green pepper.
How many slices could have more than one item on them?

FINISHING OFF

Karl needs ribbon to bind the edges of his quilt. He needs 200 cm for the sides and 128 cm for the top and bottom. How many metres of ribbon should he buy?

THE PENNY KICK

Nadia kicked a penny closer to 3.2 m than to 3.3 m. How far might she have kicked the penny?

MORE DESSERT

After his big party, Damien has pie left over. He has more than $3\frac{1}{2}$ pies, but less than 4 pies. How much might he have?

Make up other problems. Post them on the bulletin board for your classmates to solve.

Solving a Problem by Drawing a Diagram

Try this problem before going on.

WHAT'S THE SHAPE?

This triangle is half of a bigger triangle.

The bigger triangle is $\frac{1}{3}$ of an even bigger shape.
What is the biggest shape?

Saad solved the problem by drawing a diagram.

I made the bigger triangle by flipping the original one.
I cut out the bigger triangle and traced it 3 times.
My biggest shape looks like a trapezoid.

Did you find a shape that was different from Saad's?

Work with a partner.

Solve these problems by drawing a diagram.

GEOBOARDS

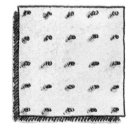

Find at least 6 different ways to divide this geoboard into fourths.

IN TOUCH

100 students are going to take part in a spell-a-thon. 5 students each phone 5 others to tell them when it's being held. Use a decimal to describe what fraction of students know when to come.

FIREWOOD

A camper can cut a log into fourths in 12 minutes. How long would it take him to cut a log the same size into sixths?

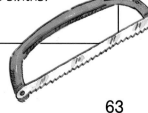

Use models or diagrams to show each of these amounts.

1. $\frac{1}{3}$ of a 12-sticker strip

2. $\frac{1}{3}$ of a 6-sticker strip

3. $\frac{4}{9}$ of a quilt square

4. $\frac{3}{8}$ of a pizza

5. 0.17 of a hundredths grid

6. pattern blocks showing $3\frac{1}{6}$

Solve these problems.

7. A bag contains 20 marbles. How many bags are used to get 70 marbles?

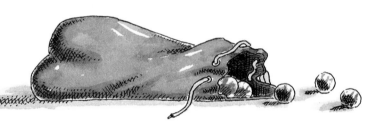

8. 10 students from each class take part in the science fair. Mr. Tyler's class has 30 students. Ms. Wilke's class has 10 students. Mrs. Montesano's class has 20 students. Which class had the greatest fraction of students taking part? the least fraction?

9. A group of 100 students takes music. 60 students are girls and 40 are boys. 15 students wear glasses and 85 do not. 35 are under age 9 and 65 are not. Use decimals to describe the group in at least four ways.

10. Keith has $1.60. Sal has a dollar and 2 quarters. Who has more? How much more?

Play each game with a partner.

Compare Pairs

- Shuffle and deal all the cards.
- Each turn over your top card. The player with the greater decimal takes both cards.
- If the decimals are equal, turn over your next cards and compare them. The player with the greater decimal takes all 4 cards.
- Continue until all the cards are turned up. The player with the most cards wins.

Example

This player ↑
takes the cards.

0.35	0.53	0.50	0.5	0.55	0.03	0.30	0.3	0.32	0.25
1.50	1.5	1.25	1.52	1.23	1.02	1.20	1.2	1.55	1.35
5.75	7.35	7.25	7.52	2.70	2.7	2.07	2.53	3.30	3.03

Build the Tower

- Roll the dice.
- Choose one number as the denominator of your fraction. The numerator is always 1.
- The second number tells how many counters you can use to cover your fraction on your Tower Mat.
- Take turns. The first player to completely cover her or his mat wins.

Example

 Choose $\frac{1}{6}$.

1				
$\frac{1}{2}$		$\frac{1}{2}$		
$\frac{1}{3}$	$\frac{1}{3}$		$\frac{1}{3}$	
$\frac{1}{4}$	$\frac{1}{4}$		$\frac{1}{4}$	$\frac{1}{4}$
$\frac{1}{5}$	$\frac{1}{5}$	$\frac{1}{5}$	$\frac{1}{5}$	$\frac{1}{5}$
●	●	●	$\frac{1}{6}$ $\frac{1}{6}$ $\frac{1}{6}$	

Take Your Pick

BIG E, LITTLE E

Use a hundredths grid.
Draw and color an E on the grid so that more than 0.30 of the grid is colored.
Now draw an E where less than 0.30 of the grid is colored.

LOOSE CHANGE

Betty has 12 coins – dimes, quarters, and dollars.
More than $\frac{1}{2}$ of the coins are quarters.
Less than $\frac{1}{4}$ of the coins are dollars.
What coins might she have?
Is there another solution?

WORD PUZZLES

Choose a word that has 10 letters. Write the decimal that tells
- how many letters are vowels,
- how many letters are in the first half of the alphabet.

Give both decimal clues to a classmate. Can the person guess your word?

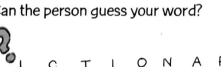
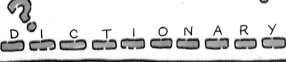

FIND THE WHOLE

This rectangle is $\frac{3}{2}$ of the basic shape.
What's the basic shape?

MORE COOKIES

A cookie recipe calls for 1 cup of sugar and makes 30 cookies. Michel increases the recipe to get more cookies. He uses $1\frac{1}{2}$ cups of sugar.
How many cookies does he make?

Make up other problems. Post them on the bulletin board for your classmates to solve.

1. A book has 10 chapters. Hans has read 7 chapters. What fraction of the book has he still to read?

2. Paper comes in packs of 100 sheets. How many packs must you buy to get 750 sheets?

3. Find three other names for 0.8.

4. Find two other names for $\frac{2}{4}$.

5. Cheryl's family has 5 people. What can the smallest fraction be that tells how many females are in her family?
What can the largest fraction be for the number of females?

6. Six slices of one pizza is less pizza than 3 slices of another. How is that possible?

7. Claudio said he ordered these cards from the smallest number to the largest. Richard says he made a mistake.
Who is right? Why?

$\frac{1}{2}$ $\frac{3}{5}$ $\frac{5}{4}$ 0.7   1   1.6

8. If it's 9:30 now, what time will it be in $1\frac{1}{2}$ hours?

9. Draw a diagram to show why another name for $3\frac{1}{3}$ is $\frac{10}{3}$.

10. Ms. Coggins gave some students a strip of 20 stickers to share. Betty took $\frac{1}{5}$ of the strip, Danielle took $\frac{1}{4}$, Matthew took $\frac{2}{5}$, and Emily got the rest. How many stickers did each student get? Tell how they could share the strip fairly.

Thinking Back

What fraction do you find easiest to change to a decimal? Why? Ask several classmates the same questions. Write about what you find out.

$$\frac{8}{3} \quad \frac{9}{5} \quad \frac{13}{4}$$

Tell what you know about these fractions.

These decimals have the same number of tenths. Tell how you would find which is greatest.

3.45   1.49   2.44   0.48

Which do you think is easier, finding the greater of two fractions or of two decimals? Write to a friend telling why you think so.

My pizza is cut in half, but I have 5 friends. What do I do?

Tell Abi what to do.

What questions do you still have about fractions and decimals?

Investigating Food Packages

Food comes in many different types of packages.
How are the packages different? Why do you think they're different?
What types of food packages does your family buy?

WHAT Data Can We Collect About Packages?

Amy found these packages in her kitchen.

Amy's Tally Chart

Cardboard	++++ ++++ ++++ ++++ IIII
Metal	++++ III
Glass	++++ ++++ ++++ ++++
Plastic	++++ I
Paper	II
Other	III

1. How many packages did she find?

2. In the pictograph, why are one and a half boxes colored to show the plastic packages?

3. In the bar graph, why is the bar for cardboard packages 24 squares high?
   What heights are the other bars?

4. Compare the categories in Amy's data. Make a statement about 2 categories, for example, metal packages and cardboard.

5. Which graph do you find easiest to understand? Why?

Work in a group.

6. Collect your own data about food packages. Graph it. Then make up problems about your graphs for another group to solve.

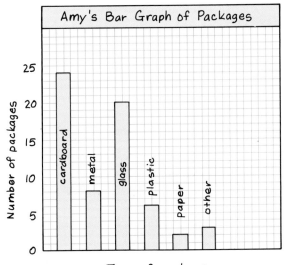

Amy's Pictograph

Cardboard	☐ ☐ ☐ ☐ ☐ ☐
Metal	☐ ☐
Glass	☐ ☐ ☐ ☐ ☐
Plastic	☐ ☐
Paper	☐
Other	☐

☐ represents 4 packages

Amy's Bar Graph of Packages

Number of packages

25
20
15
10
5
0

cardboard · metal · glass · plastic · paper · other

Type of package

Did You Know...?

In 1992, about three quarters of the boxes used for products like cereals, pasta, and cake mixes were made of recycled paper and cardboard.

▶ What fraction of your food packages have these symbols?

 Recyclable

 Recycled

How Can We Measure Food Packages?

The height of the 2 L pop bottle is about 30 cm. Estimate the actual heights of the other 6 packages.

Work in a group.

1. Choose 9 packages.
   Estimate each distance up and down and across.
   Then check. How close were your estimates?

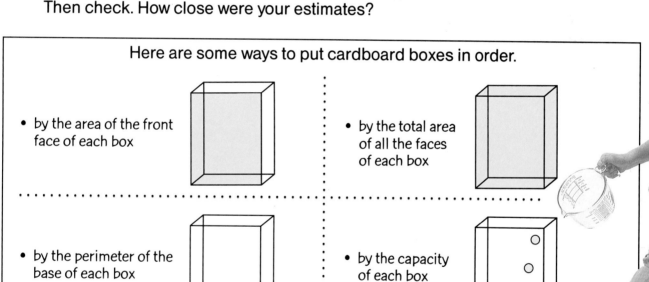

Here are some ways to put cardboard boxes in order.

- by the area of the front face of each box

- by the total area of all the faces of each box

- by the perimeter of the base of each box

- by the capacity of each box

2. Choose one way to order 9 boxes from greatest to least.
   Try another way. Are the boxes in the same order each time?
   Can you find two measurements that will give you the same order?

Did you Know...?

On the average, each household in Canada put out about 1.8 kg of trash per day in 1991!

▶ About how much garbage do you and your family throw out in a week?

How Can We Make Packages from Nets?

1. Look at the packages in your classroom. Which shapes are most common? Is one shape common for a certain type of product? Why might this be?

2. Look at the photos. If you could fold up each net, what shape of box would you see? How many faces would each box have? edges? corners?

3. Choose a box from the packages in your classroom.
   Trace its faces to create a net.
   Cut out the net and try to fold it up.
   Does it work?

HOW Can We Find the Best Buy?

---

1. Does the type of container or package affect the price? Explain.

$1.49	$2.00
1.36 L	1.36 L

$1.15	$1.15	$2.09
1 kg	1 kg	2 kg

$2.59	$3.69
540 mL	568 mL

---

2. Is the largest container or package the best buy? Explain.

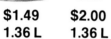

$1.59	$3.69	$3.09
1 L	4 L	2 L

$1.89	$2.89	$3.89
250 mL	500 mL	750 mL

$4.49	$12.99	$2.29
2.5 kg	10 kg	1 kg

$4.39	$6.29	$2.99
750 g	1 kg	500 g

73

Silly Cylinders

Is the distance around the base of a can less than the height? Always?

Depends How You Look at It

About how much space do 100 tuna cans take up?

Got You Covered

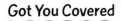

About how many burgers will a one-litre bottle of ketchup cover?

Going Crackers

About how much does 1 cracker cost?

Christie Crackers
450 g $2.39

Now investigate using another type of cracker.

Breton Crackers
225 g $3.89

What Went Wrong?

In a box of instant oatmeal there are 10 packets. Each weighs 36 g. The outside of the box says the entire contents weigh 325 g. What's wrong?

Make up your OWN investigation. Then post it on the bulletin board for others to try.

Thinking Back

Harry's Pictograph

over 500 g

250 g - 500 g

under 250 g

$\square$ = ? packages

Tell what you know about the masses of Harry's packages.

Two cereal boxes have different heights. Explain why they might still contain the same amount of cereal.

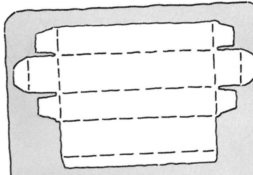

Describe what the package looks like when you fold this net.

What do you need to know to decide the length of the shelves that will hold 100 boxes of cereal?

What else would you like to know about food packages? Tell what you would do to find out.

75

Examining

▼ How many pieces of macaroni are there altogether?

two hundred thirty-six

600

100 100 100

About how many pieces of macaroni would a cup hold? ▶

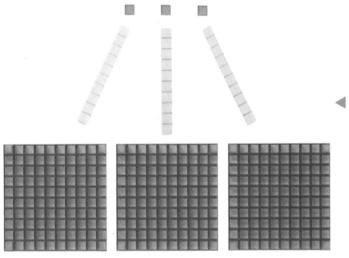

◀ How many are in each row?
What number pattern do you see?
Which base ten blocks would you put in the next row to continue the pattern?

Number Situations

Each large square on the tablecloth ▶
has 25 small squares.
How many small squares are in
1 row of large squares?
the whole tablecloth?
How long would the tablecloth be
if it had 1000 small squares?

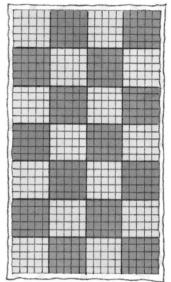

big-screen TV

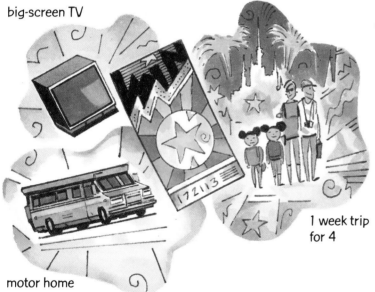

1 week trip
for 4

motor home

◀ Estimate how much each prize
is worth.
Which do you think is the
first prize? second? third?
Why?

Tell how this rhyme would change if every number ▶
became 1000 times as great.

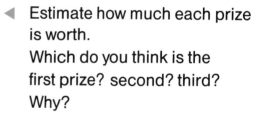

There were ten in the bed
And the little one said,
"Roll over! Roll over!"
So they all rolled over
And one fell out . . .

How much money would you have if you had 1 more of each bill?

Building Number Towers

Alex's class is building number towers.
Each layer must be full before a new layer is started.

If Alex placed a unit beside the rod, what would you name this tower?

Work in a group.

Use base ten blocks.

NAMES

one thousand one hundred ten
1 thousand + 1 hundred + 1 ten
1000 + 100 + 10
1110

1. Build 2 different towers that have the same height as Alex's. Name them.
   How many different towers could you build that have the same height?

2. Build these towers.
   Write different names for each one.

- a tower made from one large cube, two flats, and some rods

- a tower about half the height of three large cubes

Make predictions. Then build the towers to check.

3. How many large cubes do you need to build a tower named 10 000? How tall would it be in centimetres?

4. How would you name a tower about as tall as you are?

5. How could you build a tower named 50 000 using only flats?

6. Why are the towers named 99 ? 3 and 99 ? 7 the same height no matter what the missing digits are?

7. How can you tell which of these towers is the tallest?

   12 345   12 780   12 860

8. Which blocks would you move to make these towers the same height?

   2400   1800

   Name the 2 new towers.

9. Which tower can you build with the least number of blocks?

   5000   145   27

10. Build 2 towers where the shorter one uses more blocks than the taller one. Name them.

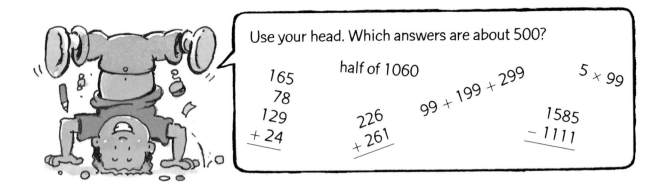

Use your head. Which answers are about 500?

165
78
129
+ 24

half of 1060

226
+ 261

99 + 199 + 299

5 × 99

1585
− 1111

Counting People

Canada has many places with small populations.

	Population (in a recent year)					
	Thousands					
	H	T	O	H	T	O
Bella Coola, British Columbia				8	8	9
Peace River, Alberta			6	2	8	8
La Ronge, Saskatchewan			2	6	9	6
Portage la Prairie, Manitoba			7	2	3	3
Fort Erie, Ontario		2	3	2	5	3
Chicoutimi, Quebec		6	1	0	8	3
Grand Falls, New Brunswick			6	2	0	9
Yarmouth, Nova Scotia			7	6	1	7
Kensington, Prince Edward Island			1	2	4	9
Corner Brook, Newfoundland		2	2	7	1	9
Whitehorse, Yukon Territories		1	5	1	9	9
Coppermine, North West Territories				8	8	8

We read the population of Whitehorse as
fifteen thousand one hundred ninety-nine.
We write 15 199.

1. Write and read each population greater than Whitehorse's.

80

Use the place value chart.

2. Which places have populations between 1000 and 10 000?

3. If a family moves to Whitehorse, what might the new population be?

4. Which place has a population closest to the population in your area?

5. How many more than 60 thousand people live in Chicoutimi?

6. Which places have populations less than 3000?
How many more people must move to each town to make its population three thousand?
Tell what you did.

7. Which places have populations that differ by 500 or less?

Use a reference book about your province.

8. Find a place with a population between those of Whitehorse and Corner Brook.

9. Name some places in your province that could be villages, towns, and cities.

10. Make up some problems about populations of places in your province for others to solve.

Ontario Population

In Ontario, a place is called a village if it has at least 500 people, a town if it has at least 2000 people, or a city if it has at least 15 000 people.

Four out of five Ontarians live in cities and towns. Ontario has more than 30 cities with populations greater than 50 000, including Canada's largest city, Toronto.

What is the tenth number in this pattern?

25, 45, 65, 85, 105, . . .

Make up your own pattern.

Estimating with Fasteners

About how many staples are there in a strip 1 m long?

Pascal counted 19 staples in a strip 1 cm long.

That's about 20 staples in every centimetre.

Holly read on the box that there are 210 staples in a regular strip.

The strip measures 10.6 cm. So there are about 200 staples in 10 cm.

Use a metre stick and complete both Pascal's and Holly's methods.

Work in a group.

1. How many boxes of 5000 staples do you need to have 10 000? 25 000? 99 000?

2. About how far would the strips in a box of staples reach if they were all lined up in a row?

Choose one of these estimation problems.
Collect the information you need.
Write about what you did to get an estimate.

Or make up your own.

3. Which has a greater mass, 1000 elastic bands or 1000 tacks?

4. About how many handfuls of safety pins do you need to get more than 10 000?

5. About how long a chain can you make with a box of paper clips?

COUNT ON IT

How long do you think it would take to count to 99 999?
How could you find out?

99 997, 99 998, 99 99...

BUG SCREEN

About how many holes would there be in an area the size of your math book?

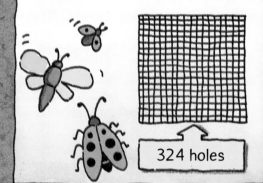

324 holes

GREATEST AND LEAST

How many different 5-digit numbers can you create using the digits 3, 3, 5, 5, and 0?
Which is the greatest number? the least number?

NUMBER STAIRCASE

5
30
300
4000
20 000

Add all the numbers.
What do you notice about the answer?
Does it matter if you add up or down?
Build a number staircase that has a sum between 40 000 and 50 000.

HAIRY PROBLEM

Most people have about 100 000 hairs on their head. Explain why there must be at least 2 people in Calgary with the same number of hairs.

Make up other problems. Post them on the bulletin board for your classmates to solve.

Are there more odd-numbered pages or even-numbered pages in this book?

Using Number Codes

Creating Numbers for Different Purposes

Each member of the Rainy Day Club has a number that fits this code.

Rainy Day Club Code
- between ten thousand and twenty thousand
- even
- at least one 0

1. Which of these numbers can be used?

   53 330   9999   11 126   10 001   10 456

2. What is the least possible number that fits the code? the greatest possible number?

Work in a group.

Use a place value chart.

3. Write one number for the Magicians' Club. Then find the least and greatest numbers.

Magicians' Club Code
- between 20 000 and 60 000
- each digit is even
- sum of digits is 10

4. Find the least and greatest number for each code. Then find 3 numbers that fit both codes.

Inventors' Club Code
- between 10 and 20
- 2 decimal places
- hundredths digit > tenths digit

Mystery Club Code
- 4 digits
- sum of 2 decimal digits is 10

5. Create your own number code for a club. Make up problems about it for classmates to solve.

Do these in your head.

| 9 + 30 + 800 |
| 7000 + 500 + 80 + 1 |
| 769 − 60 |
| 6439 − 6000 |
| 8952 − 50 |

Would it be faster to use a calculator?

Finding Calculator Patterns

BUTTERFLY FLIGHT

On Monday a butterfly flew 1 m.
On Tuesday it flew 10 times as far as on Monday.
On Wednesday it flew 10 times as far as on Tuesday.
On what day will it fly 10 000 m?

Josie looked for a pattern to solve this problem.

Mon	1
Tues	10
Wed	100
Thurs	
Fri	
Sat	

What might Josie have done to get the number 100?
What might she do next?
Use your calculator to solve the problem.

Work with a partner.

Use a calculator.

---

1. Continue each pattern 4 more times. What do you notice?

100 + 100 =	0.9 + 0.99 =	3 × 37 =
200 + 200 =	0.8 + 0.99 =	6 × 37 =
300 + 300 =	0.7 + 0.99 =	9 × 37 =

---

2. Continue each chain pattern 4 more times.

| 1 + 10 = | 2000 − 100 = |
| 1 + 10 + 100 = | 2000 − 100 − 100 = |

What chain pattern gives each set of results?

3. ⌐1000⌐ ⌐2000⌐ ⌐3000⌐ ⌐4000⌐

4. ⌐6225⌐ ⌐6125⌐ ⌐6025⌐ ⌐5925⌐

5. ⌐1.5⌐ ⌐11.5⌐ ⌐21.5⌐ ⌐31.5⌐

6. ⌐25⌐ ⌐75⌐ ⌐225⌐ ⌐675⌐

Use the other numbers from 1 to 8.
Arrange them so that each row and
column adds to 14.

?	?	7
5	■	?
?	?	?

Locating Decorations

Relating Numbers to Space

Some holiday decorations are placed
at road intersections.
The snowflake is 2 blocks east and
1 block north of Town Centre.
What avenue and street meet there?

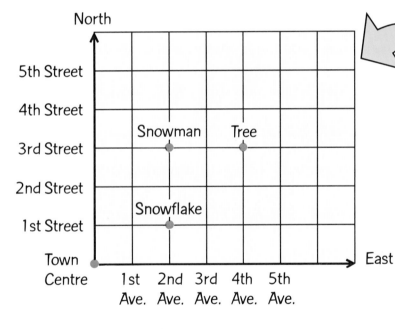

North

5th Street

4th Street

Snowman   Tree

3rd Street

2nd Street

Snowflake

1st Street

Town   East
Centre   1st   2nd   3rd   4th   5th
         Ave. Ave. Ave. Ave. Ave.

You can use ordered pairs or
coordinates (Avenue, Street) to
describe the location. Tell why
(2, 1) locates the snowflake.

1. Write the coordinates of
  • the snowman
  • the tree

2. Does it matter whether
  you use (3, 5) or (5, 3)
  to locate a decoration?
  Explain.

Use grids.

3. Locate the 3 decorations. Then locate another one
  so that all 4 form a square.
  What are its coordinates?

4. Locate each ordered pair. What pattern do you notice?
  Mark the next ordered pair.

  • (1, 1) (1, 2) (1, 3)   • (1, 2) (2, 3) (3, 4)

  Make up your own pattern.

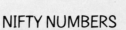
FIVE WITH FIVE

We're five numbers with five digits each.
All of us are odd numbers.
One of us is the least 5-digit number.
Another is the greatest 5-digit number.
Others have digits that add to 20, 30, and 40.
Who might we be?

NIFTY NUMBERS

Continue the pattern as far as you can.
What do you notice?
$9 + 9 =$
$99 + 99 =$
$999 + 999 =$

MOVING ZEROS

Do each step on your calculator.
What do you notice about each calculation?

$10 \times 1 = = = = = = = \div 10 = = = = = = = =$

$10 \times 1 = = = = = = = \div 10 = = = = = =$

$10 \times 1 = = = = = \div 10 = = = =$

CONNECTING DOTS

Locate each ordered pair on a grid.
Draw lines to connect them in this order.

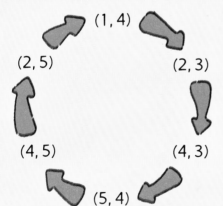

(1, 4)

(2, 5)   (2, 3)

(4, 5)   (4, 3)

(5, 4)

What shape is it?
Draw the lines of symmetry.

TELEPHONE NUMBERS

590
591
594
596
597
599

The 7-digit phone numbers in a town start with one of these. How many different telephone numbers are possible?

Make up other problems. Post them on the bulletin board for your classmates to solve.

Solving a Problem by Making a Model

Try this problem before going on.

MAKING PEANUT BUTTER

About 730 peanuts are used to make 1 kg of peanut butter.
About how many kilograms can be made with 10 000 peanuts?

Kim's group solved the problem by making a model.

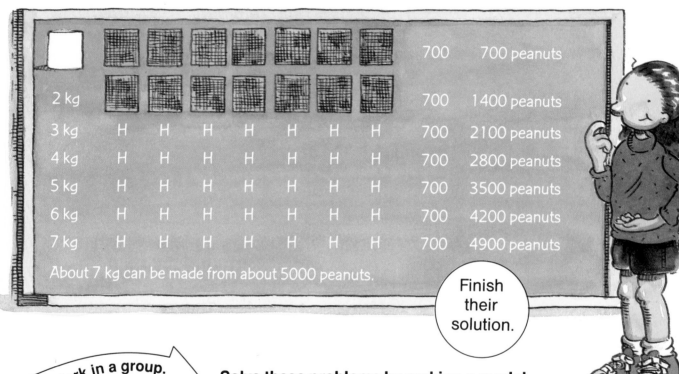

								700	700 peanuts
2 kg								700	1400 peanuts
3 kg	H	H	H	H	H	H	H	700	2100 peanuts
4 kg	H	H	H	H	H	H	H	700	2800 peanuts
5 kg	H	H	H	H	H	H	H	700	3500 peanuts
6 kg	H	H	H	H	H	H	H	700	4200 peanuts
7 kg	H	H	H	H	H	H	H	700	4900 peanuts

About 7 kg can be made from about 5000 peanuts.

Finish their solution.

Work in a group.

Solve these problems by making a model.

HAND PERIMETER

Could a person's hand have a perimeter of 1 m?

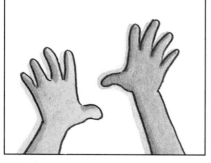

BIGGER BOXES

Make the smallest open box you can that will hold 10 pencils.
What size is the smallest open box that will hold 1000 pencils?

YOU'RE SURROUNDED

How many cubes are needed to surround 1 cube?
All faces, edges, and corners must be hidden.

Write a number for each amount.

1.

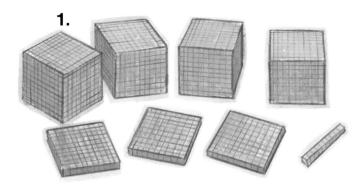

2.

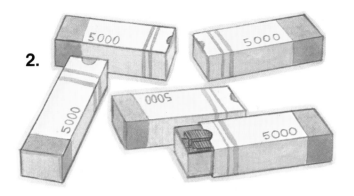

3. 10 000 + 5000 + 40 + 7

4.

date *Aug. 18/94*

PAY TO THE ORDER OF
Monarch Used Cars $

AMOUNT *thirteen thousand four hundred fifty-five*

Signature *Pat Barr*

Solve.

5. How many packages do you need to have more than 10 000 seeds?

220 seeds

6. Order the numbers from least to greatest.

12 199   13 007   12 205

Which pairs of numbers add to more than 25 000?

7. About how much money has been raised?

OUR GOAL 50 000

8. Write the next two ordered pairs to continue the pattern.

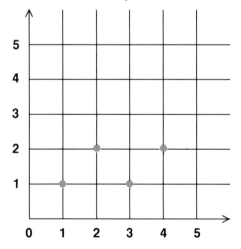

9. What are the next 4 numbers in the pattern?

9500, 10 000, 10 500, 11 000, 11 500,

10. Write a number that fits these rules.
  • between 15 000 and 16 000
  • sum of digits is even
  • hundreds digit is odd

Playing Games for Practice

Play each game in a group of 2, 3, or 4.

Choose Your Place

- Roll a die. Put that many counters in any blank column on your place value chart.
- Take turns until each player has five digits.
- The player with the greatest number wins.

Example You roll

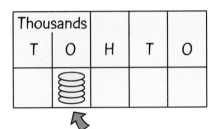

You might decide to place 5 counters here.

Variation: The player with the least number wins.

Name that Score

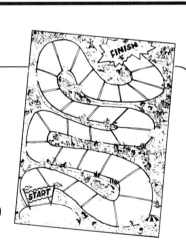

- Spin a spinner 5 times. Make a 5-digit number by recording the numbers you spin in order.
- Take turns.
  Score 1 if your number is odd
       2 if the tens digit is even
       3 if your number is between 10 000 and 20 000
- Your score is the number of spaces you move on the gameboard.

    Example In 5 turns, you spin 17 902.
           Move 5 spaces.

Variation: Make up your own scoring rules.

Take Your Pick

SPINNING NUMBERS

A number is formed by adding a number on the red spinner to a number on the green spinner.
How many numbers are possible?
Is it more likely that the number will be even or odd?

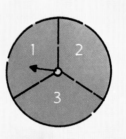

TELEPHONE BOOK PAGES

About how many pages in your local telephone book do you need to make a list of 10 000 names?

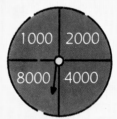

COMPUTER PRINTOUT

A computer printed out this letter pattern.
How many lines are needed to have 10 000 letters?
Name the 1000th letter.

```
A B C D E F G H I  J K L M N O P Q R S T U V W X Y
Z A B C D E F G H I  J K L M N O P Q R S T U V W X
Y Z A B C D E F G H I  J K L M N O P Q R S T U V W
X Y Z A B C D E F G H I  J K L M N O P Q R S T U V
W X Y Z A B C D E F G H I  J K L M N O P Q R S T U
```

INSTANT WEALTH

Suppose all coins became worth 100 times as much as they are now.
How much would each coin be worth?
If everyone in your class had a $1 coin, would there be more than $50 000 in all?

MISSING DIGITS

Use the other digits from 0 to 9.
No digit can be used more than once.
Fill in the missing digits to make this true.
Try it more than one way.

?? 249 > ?? 173

Make up other problems. Post them on the bulletin board for your classmates to solve.

1. Is something wrong? If so, how would you fix it?

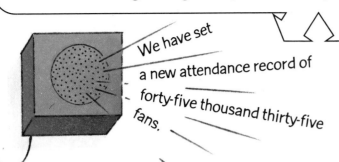

We have set a new attendance record of forty-five thousand thirty-five fans.

DAILY NEWS

New Attendance Record 4535

2. How would you write in words the price of the yacht?

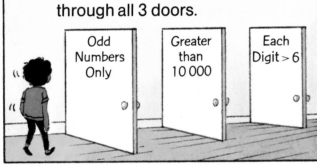

$32 456.00

3. About how many times do you think your eyes move while you're at school?

4. Write a number that can go through all 3 doors.

| Odd Numbers Only | Greater than 10 000 | Each Digit > 6 |

5. Which share would you rather have? Explain.

$\frac{1}{2}$ of

$\frac{3}{3}$ of

$\frac{1}{8}$ of

6. One dollar is worth about 1000 Lira of Italian money. How much might you pay for a hamburger if you visited Italy?

7. Locate these ordered pairs on a grid. Join them in order.

(1, 2) (1, 5) (2, 4) (3, 5) (3, 2)

What did you draw?

8. Estimate the number of holes in this ceiling tile. About how many tiles do you need to show 1000 holes?

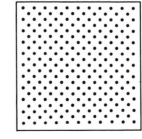

Write an interesting 5-digit number.
Tell why you think it is interesting.
Describe what your number might show or be used for.

What would you do to help someone understand the meaning of the number 10 000?

For which two numbers is it easy to find the greater?
Explain why you picked them and what you did to compare them.

10 000   9999   14 567   14 657   55 406

Think of something you have seen more than 10 000 of at one time. How do you know there were probably more than 10 000?

Write about what would happen to the numbers you know if the digit 0 disappeared and could not be used again.

POOF!   POOF!

What questions do you still have about number situations?

Extending Addition

Maple Creek School has 325 students.
Lakeshore School has 304 students.

▲

Which school has more students?
How many more?

In 1950, the average time spent watching television at home each day was 4 h 35 min.
In 1980, the average was 6 h 36 min.

▲

What was the increase?
How much does your family watch television?
Is this more or less than the average in 1980?
How much?
What do you think the average will be in 2000?

and Subtraction

◀ How much higher should the meat thermometer read for pork than for rare roast beef? for poultry than for medium roast beef?

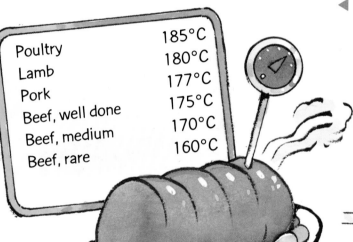

Poultry	185°C
Lamb	180°C
Pork	177°C
Beef, well done	175°C
Beef, medium	170°C
Beef, rare	160°C

9 9 9 9 . 9

▲ How many more kilometres will the car travel before the odometer shows a digit in the empty space?

What will that digit be? How many kilometres will the odometer show then?

Tell about an addition or subtraction you solved while not in school.

Which number does not belong? Why?
Write another number that would not belong
for the same reason.

3824   3257

346   3422

4236

Think of other
ways to answer.

Planning a Trip

Nicholas and Danielle's family
is driving from Halifax, NS,
to Thunder Bay, ON.

They estimated the distance
from Halifax to Fredericton
taking the ferry.

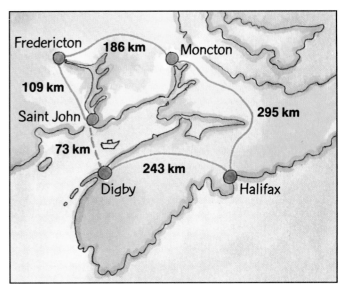

Fredericton — 186 km — Moncton

109 km

Saint John — 295 km

73 km

243 km

Digby   Halifax

Danielle estimated like this.

243 km → 200
73 km → 100
109 km → + 100
        400

It's about
400 km.

Nicholas estimated like this.

243 km → 250
73 km → 75
109 km → + 100
        425

It's about 425 km.

Explain both ways of estimating.

---

1. Use two different ways to estimate
the cost of the ferry for their family
of 2 adults and 2 children.

Digby to Saint John one-way fares	
Car	$57.00
Adult	$18.00
Child	$9.00

After they reached Québec City, they estimated how much farther it was to Montréal.

Fredericton to Québec City **591 km**
Fredericton to Montréal **818 km**

Nicholas estimated like this.

$$818 \text{ km} \rightarrow 800$$
$$591 \text{ km} \rightarrow -600$$
$$\overline{200}$$

It's about 200 km.

Danielle estimated like this.

$$591 \rightarrow 600 \rightarrow 800 \rightarrow 818$$
$$\text{about } 10 + \text{about } 200 + \text{about } 20$$
$$= 230$$

It's about 230 km.

Explain both ways of estimating.

2. From Fredericton to Thunder Bay is 2527 km.
Use two different ways to estimate the distance from Montréal to Thunder Bay.

Work with a partner.

Solve these problems by estimating.

3. From Halifax to Thunder Bay is 3041 km.
When they arrived in Ottawa, there were 1503 km left to Thunder Bay.
About how far had they already travelled?

4. At Wawa they saw a sign, 485 km to Thunder Bay.
About how far had they come from Ottawa?

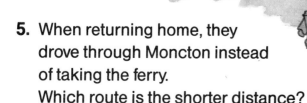

5. When returning home, they drove through Moncton instead of taking the ferry.
Which route is the shorter distance?

6. Make up two estimating problems about the trip for other pairs to solve.

97

What solid am I?

I roll.
I slide.
I have 2 faces that are circles.

Create a riddle about another solid for classmates to solve.

 aking Jewellery

Adding and Subtracting Special Whole Numbers

Mr. Cheng used 165 beads for a necklace and 98 beads for a bracelet.

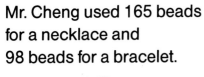

Katie is finding how many beads he used altogether.

Finish Katie's work.

$$\begin{array}{r} 165 \\ + 100 \\ \hline 265 \end{array}$$

Mr. Cheng had 352 beads for earrings. He used 99 of them. Mark is finding how many beads were left.

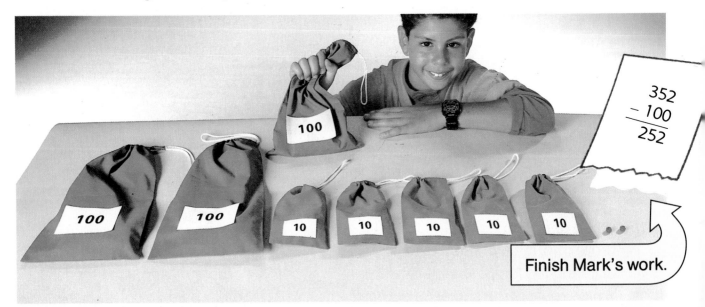

$$\begin{array}{r} 352 \\ - 100 \\ \hline 252 \end{array}$$

Finish Mark's work.

1. How many beads will be in each box?

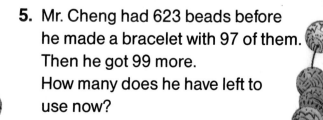

2. Do these in your head.
Make up a problem about beads for two of them.

145	235	189		278	555	407
+ 99	+ 97	+ 98		− 97	− 98	− 99

425 + 999   99 + 99 + 99   321 − 98   421 − 99

3. Mr. Cheng used 174 beads for another necklace and 99 beads for another bracelet. How many beads did he use this time?

4. A bag had 537 beads before 98 beads were made into earrings.
How many beads are left?

5. Mr. Cheng had 623 beads before he made a bracelet with 97 of them. Then he got 99 more.
How many does he have left to use now?

6. There is a total of 600 beads in 3 necklaces.
All the necklaces have about the same but not exactly the same number of beads.
How many could be in each?

99

Find the total number
of rectangles.

Selling Widgets

The National Widget
Company makes and
sells widgets.

Rosa and Neil
are finding out how
many widgets were
sold in July and
August.

National Widget Company Sales from May to December			
	Cases	Cartons	Boxes	Widgets
May	1	3	3	9
June	2	0	7	5
July	0	9	4	8
August	0	6	2	7
September	1	0	8	6
October	2	5	0	2
November	4	0	7	2
December	5	0	0	5

10 widgets in a box
10 boxes in a carton
10 cartons in a case

Rosa added the
single widgets first,
then the boxes,
then the cartons.

Neil added the
cartons first, then
the boxes, then the
single widgets.

$$\begin{array}{r} 1 \\ 948 \\ + 627 \\ \hline 5 \end{array}$$

Use base ten blocks to show how Rosa and Neil solved the problem.
Finish both additions.

What other ways can you think of?

$$\begin{array}{r} 948 \\ + 627 \\ \hline 1500 \\ 60 \end{array}$$

100

1. Use two methods to find the total sales
   - for May and June
   - for August, September, and October

Use base ten blocks.

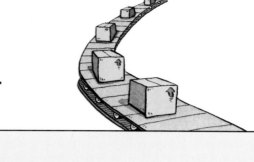

2. What could each month's sales be?
   January was more than 780.
   February was less than 830.
   March was greater than 3060.
   April was less than 2100.

   Find the total sales for
   - January and February
   - March and April

January	7	?	4
February	8	?	6
March	3 0	?	0
April	2	?	6 5

3. Calculate in your head how many parts are used
   for making widgets each day.

Use this addition to help you.

$$\begin{array}{r} 2000 \\ + 3000 \\ \hline 5000 \end{array}$$

	Monday	Tuesday	Wednesday	Thursday
Morning	2005	2500	1999	2005
Afternoon	3005	3500	2999	2999

4. Which two months had the highest sales?
   Why do you think this was so?

5. What were the total sales for the 3 lowest months?

6. Estimate how many widgets were sold in July,
   August, and September. Explain how you did it.

7. Predict how many widgets will be sold next
   January, February, and March. Explain.

8. What do you think a widget is?
   Draw a widget and describe its use.
   Make up two addition problems about widgets
   for another group to solve.

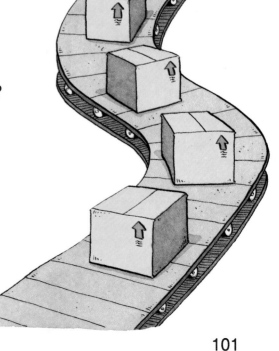

Which designs have symmetry?

Draw a rectangle with a design that has symmetry.

Pouring Water

The container has 1750 mL of water. 575 mL of water is used to make orange juice.

Marty and Lola are finding out how much water is left.

I'll trade 1 ten for 10 ones.

I'll count back from 1750.

$$\begin{array}{r} \overset{4\ 10}{\cancel{1}\cancel{7}\cancel{5}\cancel{0}} \\ -575 \\ \hline 5 \end{array}$$

$$\begin{array}{r} \overset{6\ \overset{14}{\cancel{4}}\ 10}{\cancel{1}\cancel{7}\cancel{5}\cancel{0}} \\ -575 \\ \hline 75 \end{array}$$

$$1750 - 500 = 1250$$
$$1250 - 50 = 1200$$

← Finish Marty's subtraction.   Finish Lola's subtraction. ↗

Show how Marty and Lola might solve these problems.

1. A container has 1750 mL of water. How much is left after 325 mL is used?

2. How much water is left if 1050 mL is taken from a container with 1200 mL?

Model your solutions.

3. A container has 1500 mL of water. How much is left after 875 mL is used for making lemonade?

4. 1075 mL of water is mixed with 355 mL of concentrate for pineapple juice. How many millilitres of juice are there?

5. 950 mL of water is taken from a 1750 mL container that is almost full. Estimate how much water is left in the container. Explain.

6. A container has 5000 mL of water.

   Gwenna uses 1345 mL.
   Then Ben uses 750 mL.
   Then Jamie uses 680 mL.
   Then Hal uses 1550 mL.

   Is there enough for Erika to use 800 mL? If so, how much would be left? If not, how much more is needed?

7. A 2000 mL container has 1175 mL left in it after 3 different quantities are used. How much could each quantity be?

8. Calculate in your head how much water will be left in each container.

Use this subtraction to help you.

$$\begin{array}{r} 1230 \\ -\ 650 \\ \hline 580 \end{array}$$

I need to use 640 mL.

I'm going to take out 650 mL.

I will be using 550 mL.

1230 mL   1240 mL   1230 mL

9. Make up addition and subtraction problems about water containers for another group to solve.

There are lots of ways to estimate 364 + 289.
Here are some. Can you think of any more?

1. You can add the hundreds and then estimate.

300 + 200 = 500
64 + 89 is more than 100
500 + 100 = 600   364 + 289 is more than 600

2. You might round to the nearest hundred.

364 → 400   400
289 → 300   + 300
                   700   364 + 289 is about 700

3. You could round one of the numbers to the nearest hundred and
count by hundreds.

289 is a little less than 300

364 + 300 → (364, 464, 564, 664)   364 + 289 is a little less than 664

4. You might round to the nearest 50.

364 is a little more than   350
289 is a little less than   + 300
                                   650

Work in a group.

Show two different ways
to estimate each sum.

1.	473	**2.**	3809
	+ 907		+ 1878
3.	985	**4.**	8635
	+ 74		+ 2680

5. 4705 + 1693

364 + 289 is about 650

INK BLOTS

What numbers are covered?

```
  5 7        4        4 3
+ 4 3      - 6   4    7 1
-------    --------   + 3   0
1 0 0 6    2 9 1     --------
                     1 3 3 8
```

CHANGE IT

Use 4 subtraction steps on your calculator to change the first number into the second.

| 134 → 104 |
| 568 → 8 |

SUM FUN

Different letters stand for different digits from 0 to 9.
What is the value of each letter?

```
  P I G
+ M U D
-------
  J O Y
```

CONTINUE THE PATTERN

Use your calculator to find each sum.
9 + 99
9 + 99 + 999
9 + 99 + 999 + 9999

What is the pattern?
Write the next line without using your calculator.
How far can you continue the pattern?

CHOOSING DIGITS

Use three different digits from 1 to 9 to make

- the greatest sum
- the least sum

☐ 54 + 3 ☐ 2 + 14 ☐

Make up other problems. Post them on the bulletin board for your classmates to solve.

How many blocks are in
this pyramid pattern?

What about one that starts
with 5 rows of 5 blocks?

Displaying Murals

Students painted these murals about recycling.
One mural is 4.32 m long. Another is 5.67 m long.
Lois and Conrad estimated the total length
of the murals.

Lois estimated like this.

$4.32\text{ m} \to 4$
$5.67\text{ m} \to \underline{+\,6}$
$\phantom{5.67\text{ m} \to +\,}10$

It's about 10 m.

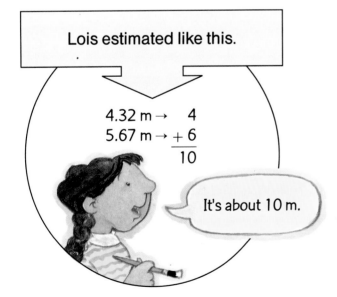

Explain Lois's method.

Conrad estimated like this.

4 and 32 hundredths
$\underline{+\text{ 5 and 67 hundredths}}$
9 and almost 1 m more

It's about 10 m.

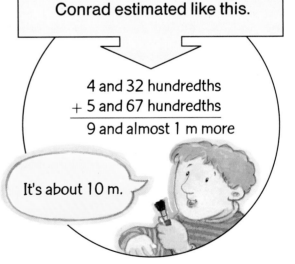

Explain Conrad's method.

1. Use two methods to estimate the total length for two murals about
   4.55 m long and 7.24 m long.

106

The wall is 16.75 m long.
A mural 8.08 m long is put on this wall.
About how much wall space is left for
other murals?

Conrad estimated like this.	Lois estimated like this.

16.75 m → 17
8.08 m → − 8
$\overline{9}$

There's about
9 m left.

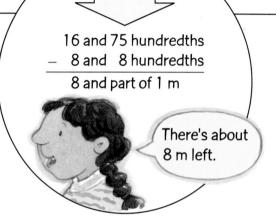

16 and 75 hundredths
− 8 and 8 hundredths
$\overline{\text{8 and part of 1 m}}$

There's about
8 m left.

Explain Conrad's method.   Explain Lois's method.

2. Use two methods to estimate the difference in length between murals
3.52 m long and 2.34 m long.

Estimate to solve.

3. Jason's mural is 6.02 m long.
It is about 4 m longer than Becky's.
How long could Becky's mural be?
Explain.

4. A wall is 14.37 m long.
Would murals 3.75 m, 5.28 m,
and 5.74 m long fit? Explain.

5. One mural is 3.25 m long.
What might the length of a second one be if 8 m
is a better estimate for the total length than 7 m? Explain.

6. Make up two estimating problems using decimal measurements
to trade with other pairs.

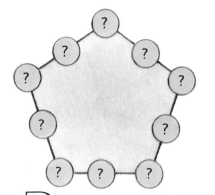

Fill the circles with the numbers 1 to 10 so that each side of the pentagon has a sum of 14.

Raising Money

Adding and Subtracting Special Decimals

Keiko's class is selling magician's equipment to raise money for class trips. They made this advertising flyer.

$3.97

$3.99

$2.99 each

$0.99

$12.98

$2.98

$1.98 each

$5.99

$10.97

$2.97

$8.99

$0.98 each

$1.99

$6.98

Keiko is finding the cost of a mask and a magic wand.

A mask costs $2.99.	1¢ less than $3
A wand costs $1.98.	2¢ less than $2
The total cost is	3¢ less than $5

What is the total cost?

1. Find the total cost of a pair of gloves and a wig.

108

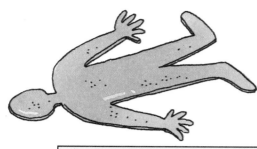

Here she is finding the change after buying a fake shadow with a $10.00 bill.

A shadow costs $6.98.   2¢ less than $7
$7 is $3 less than $10.

What is the change?

2. Find the change from a $5 bill for each purchase.

· a scarf

· a mustache and a beard

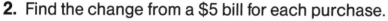

Work in a group.   **Try to solve these in your head.**

3. What is the total cost?
   · a rabbit puppet and a top hat
   · a shadow and a mask
   · a magic wand, a mask, and a scarf

4. How much is the change from a $20 bill for each of these?
   · a pair of gloves
   · a magician's cape
   · cards and 2 sets of magic pens

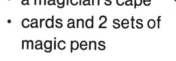

5. Choose 3 things on the flyer. What is the total cost?

6. Choose 2 things on the flyer. How much would you have left from $25.00?

7. Make up other problems about the flyer for other groups to solve.

Draw some squares on dot paper.
Cut off the corners.
What shapes can you make?

Buying Baking Goods

Try this problem before going on.

RAFI'S BAKERY

Rafi is buying 3.49 kg of chocolate sprinkles and 4.75 kg of coconut.

What is the total mass of Rafi's cake decorations?

Simon grouped the hundredths first, then the tenths, then the ones.

Use decimal models to show how Simon solved the problem.
Finish Simon's addition.

$$
\begin{array}{r}
\overset{1\ \ 1}{} \\
3.49 \\
+ \ 4.75 \\
\hline
24
\end{array}
$$

Zoe counted on from 3.49 kg starting with the whole kilograms.

3.49 + 4 = 7.49

7.49 + 0.7 = 8.19

8.19 + 0.05 = 8.24

4.75

Explain Zoe's addition.

Show how Simon and Zoe might find these sums.

1. 5.2 kg + 8.1 kg

2. 1.37 kg and 0.48 kg

Which method do you prefer? Why?

110

Model your solutions.

3. What is the total mass of each pair of bags?

Use this addition to help you.

$$1.49 \\ + 5.83 \\ \overline{7.32}$$

2.49 kg   6.83 kg   2.49 kg   4.83 kg   0.49 kg   3.83 kg

4. Find the total mass of these packages.

▶ peanut butter chips and butterscotch chips

▶ raisins and walnuts

▶ any three packages of chips

Walnuts 2.45 kg

Mint chips 2.07 kg

Raisins 3.15 kg

Chocolate chips 2.38 kg

Orange chips 1.98 kg

Peanut butter chips 0.83 kg

Coconut 0.90 kg

Pecans 1.76 kg

Butterscotch chips 1.39 kg

5. What is the total mass of 3.5 kg of brown sugar and 2.8 kg of white sugar?

6. Choose four packages. What is the total mass?

7. Two bags have a total mass the same as the raisins. What are they?

8. Make up two addition problems about these packages for another pair to solve.

111

Use a calculator to continue these patterns.

1, 2, 4, 8, ?, ?, ?, ?, ?, ?, ?

3, 6, 12, 24, ?, ?, ?, ?, ?, ?, ?

Create number patterns for classmates to continue.

Shopping at a Garage Sale

Heli has $4.92 to spend at a garage sale.
She is buying a game and wants to know how much she will have left.

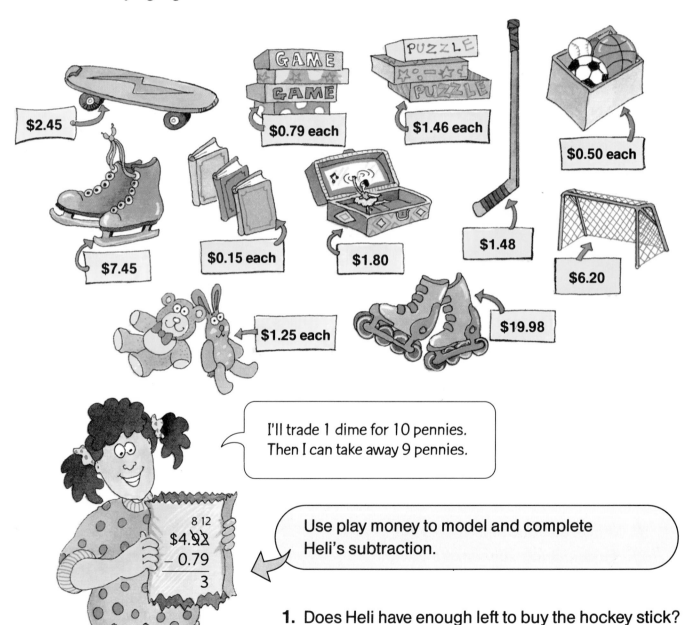

$2.45

$0.79 each

$1.46 each

$0.50 each

$7.45

$0.15 each

$1.80

$1.48

$6.20

$1.25 each

$19.98

I'll trade 1 dime for 10 pennies.
Then I can take away 9 pennies.

8 12
$4.9̸2̸
− 0.79
3

Use play money to model and complete
Heli's subtraction.

1. Does Heli have enough left to buy the hockey stick?
   If so, how much would she have left?
   If not, how much more does she need?

112

Pete is finding out how much change he will have from a $10 bill if he buys the skateboard.

I'll count on from $2.45.

$2.45 to $2.50 is 5¢.
$2.50 to $3.00 is 50¢.
$3.00 to $10.00 is $7.00.

Show how Pete can finish counting on.

Work with a partner.

Use play money or decimal models.

2. Explain how this subtraction can help Jeff and Heather find out how much they will have left.

I have $3.35 and I want to buy a puzzle at the garage sale.

$$\begin{array}{r} 335 \\ -\ 146 \\ \hline 189 \end{array}$$

I am going to buy a puzzle. I have $2.35.

3. Kyle bought a game with $1.25 and had 46¢ left.
How does this help you find how much is left after buying a game with each of these amounts?

$$\begin{array}{r} \$1.25 \\ -\ 0.79 \\ \hline \$0.46 \end{array}$$ $2.25 $10.25

$1.55

4. Which item costs the most? How much change would you get if you paid for it with a $20 bill?

5. What is the change from buying a ball with a $5 bill?

6. Maureen got $2.55 change when she bought one thing and paid with a $10 bill.
What did she buy?

7. Write problems about a garage sale for other pairs to solve.

8. You have $5.56. Choose what you would like to buy.
Do you have enough money?
If so, how much change will you get?
If not, how much more money do you need?

Adding Decimals

There are lots of ways to calculate $3.75 + 2.50$.
Here are some. Can you think of any more?

(1.) You could use a money model.

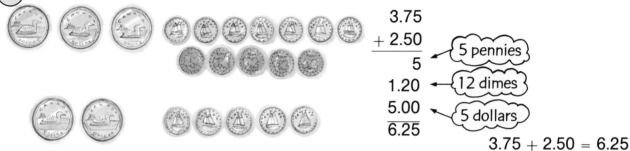

$$3.75$$
$$+ 2.50$$
$$\overline{5}$$ ← 5 pennies
$$1.20$$ ← 12 dimes
$$5.00$$ ← 5 dollars
$$\overline{6.25}$$

$$3.75 + 2.50 = 6.25$$

(2.) You might use an abacus.

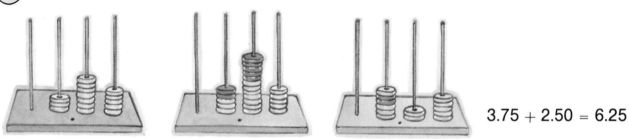

$$3.75 + 2.50 = 6.25$$

(3.) You could add the ones first, then tenths, and then hundredths.

$$3.75$$
$$+ 2.50$$
$$\overline{5.00}$$
$$6.20$$
$$6.25$$

$$3.75 + 2.50 = 6.25$$

(4.) You might add too little and then add more.

$$3.50 + 2.50 = 6.00$$
and 0.25 more $\rightarrow 6.25$

$$3.75 + 2.50 = 6.25$$

Work in a group.

Show two different ways to do each addition.

1. 4.50	**2.**	27.5
$+ 2.35$		$+ 57.9$

3. 4.27	**4.**	9.05
$+ 4.36$		$+ 3.50$

5. $13.46 + 23.61$

Subtracting Decimals

There are lots of ways to calculate 20.00 − 4.97. Here are some. Can you think of any more?

1. You could use a money model.

  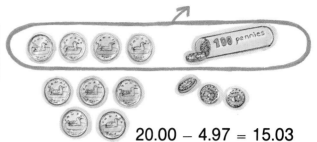

20.00 − 4.97 = 15.03

2. You might use an abacus.

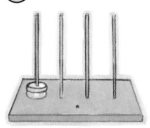  

20.00 − 4.97 = 15.03

3. You could count back.

20 − 4 = 16
   16 − 0.97 = 15.03

20.00 − 4.97 = 15.03

4. You might subtract too much and then add some back.

4.97 is 0.03 less than 5.00

$$\begin{array}{r} 20.00 \\ -\ 5.00 \\ \hline 15.00 \end{array}$$

$$\begin{array}{r} 15.00 \\ +\ 0.03 \\ \hline 15.03 \end{array}$$

20.00 − 4.97 = 15.03

 **Work in a group.**

Show two different ways to do each subtraction.

1. $\begin{array}{r} 8.50 \\ -\ 2.15 \end{array}$ **2.** $\begin{array}{r} 7.97 \\ -\ 4.28 \end{array}$

3. $\begin{array}{r} 23.46 \\ -\ 11.09 \end{array}$ **4.** $\begin{array}{r} 8.25 \\ -\ 4.25 \end{array}$

5. 31.40 − 12.96

Take Your Pick

CHANGING DIGITS

1.65
+ 8.09

Change 1 digit in each number
so the sum is 10.
Try to find more than one solution.

ARRANGING TABLES

1.5 m

Put 5 of these square tables
together so that
the perimeter is 18 m.

RIDES AT THE FAIR

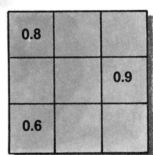

Ferris Wheel $1.25
The Screamer $1.50
Topsy-Turvy $1.75

How many rides can you
take for $13.00?

MAGIC SQUARE

0.8		
		0.9
0.6		

Each row, column, and
diagonal adds up to 1.5.

Use 0.1, 0.2, 0.3, 0.4, 0.5,
and 0.7 to complete the
magic square.

SPEEDY MATH

What's the perimeter of this park?
Find a way to do it in your head.

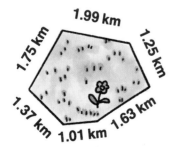

1.99 km
1.75 km
1.25 km
1.37 km
1.01 km
1.63 km

**Make up other problems. Post
them on the bulletin board for
your classmates to solve.**

Solving a Problem by Finding Missing Information

Discuss this problem before going on.

ADOPT AN ANIMAL

How much does it cost to adopt an animal at the zoo?

How can you raise the money?

Sheila's class solved the problem by asking for information and making decisions.

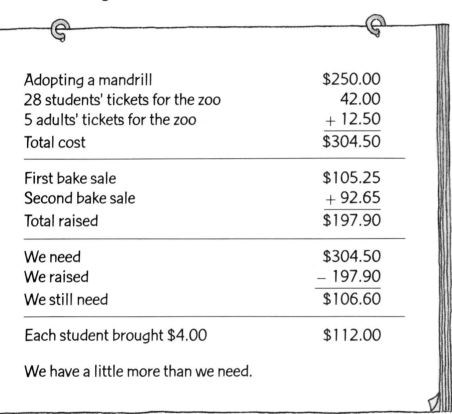

Adopting a mandrill	$250.00
28 students' tickets for the zoo	42.00
5 adults' tickets for the zoo	+ 12.50
Total cost	$304.50
First bake sale	$105.25
Second bake sale	+ 92.65
Total raised	$197.90
We need	$304.50
We raised	− 197.90
We still need	$106.60
Each student brought $4.00	$112.00

We have a little more than we need.

I phoned the zoo to ask about adopting a baboon.
We chose the mandrill because of its colors.
Then we decided to plan a class trip to visit the mandrill.

Work in a group.

Discuss how to find the information needed to solve these problems.

PLANNING LUNCH

What would a special lunch for your class cost?

GOING TO A MOVIE

How much would it cost for your class to go to a movie together?

WATCHING TV

How many hours of television do the students in your class watch each month?

Practising What You've Learned

Complete ONLY if the answer is greater than 500 but less than 1000.

1.　1995
　　 − 696

2.　 213.4
　　 + 342.1

3.　 893.7
　　 − 256.4

4.　 423.5
　　 + 31.8

Write a problem for three of these. Then solve.

5.　 265
　　 + 750

6.　 1992
　　 − 1897

7.　 4.9
　　 + 5.6

8. $10.00
　　 − 7.99

Solve.

9. Anna delivered 528 flyers.
Tony delivered 414 flyers.
How many more must they
deliver to finish the pack of 1000?

10. Myra's bike repairs cost $17.85.
She paid with a $20 bill.
How much change did she
receive?

11. Jacob entered a 10 km race.
He stopped after running 6.5 km.
How much farther would he have
to go to finish?

12. Estimate whether a 50 m roll
of fencing would fit around
this garden.

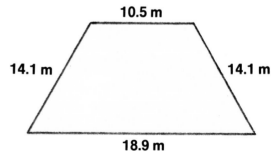

10.5 m

14.1 m　　14.1 m

18.9 m

13. Owen jumped 1.41 m.
Kachina jumped 0.09 m
farther than Owen.
How far did Kachina jump?

Playing Games for Practice

Play each game in a group of 2, 3, or 4.

Spill the Beans

100	200	300	400	500
50	150	250	350	450
30	130	230	330	430
70	170	270	370	470
100	200	300	400	500

- Spill 5 beans or counters on the gameboard.
- Add the numbers on the white squares where the beans land.
- Add the numbers on the shaded squares where the beans land.
- Subtract the lesser sum from the greater sum.
- Your score is the difference.
- Take 5 turns. The winner is the player with the highest score.

Variation: Score 0 if your difference is a multiple of 100, 1 if it is not.

Example

```
  300        130        830
  230       + 70      - 200
+ 300        200        630
  830
```

Score 630 points.

Backward Roll

- Take turns to roll a die. The player with the highest number starts the game.
- Start with a score of 10.
- Roll the die and read the number as a decimal.
- Subtract the decimal from 10 and record your score.
- Take turns. The first player with less than 1 wins.

Example

means you must subtract 0.5.

```
  10.0
 - 0.5
   9.5
```

Variation: Use 2 dice and read the numbers as a two-digit decimal.

1. A relay team has 4 runners.
   In a race, Harold's time is 4.3 s,
   Zoe's is 4.1 s, and Ivan's is 3.9 s.
   The time for the team is 16.5 s.
   What is the time for the other runner?

2. Find two numbers that are about halfway between the flags.

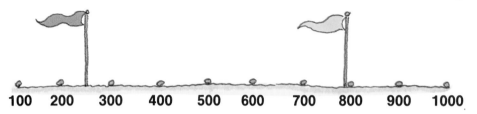

100   200   300   400   500   600   700   800   900   1000

3. Change each 6 to an 8.
   Is the number larger or smaller? By how much?

36 560

4. Tell how you estimate how much
   more one baseball glove costs
   than the other.

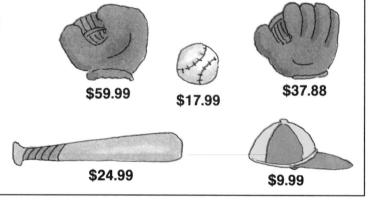

$59.99 $17.99 $37.88

5. Write a problem about this
   baseball equipment for a
   classmate to solve.

$24.99 $9.99

6. Susie owns about $\frac{1}{4}$ of these
   tennis balls.
   How many could she own?

7. Write an addition question
   with the sum 6.27.
   Write a subtraction question
   with the difference 6.27.

8. The perimeter of Joe's equilateral
   triangle is 51 cm.
   Paula drew a triangle with each side
   2 cm shorter than Joe's.
   What is the perimeter of
   Paula's triangle?

You have $5.00 to buy markers. Choose two and explain how to find the change.

$0.79 EACH

$1.25 EACH

$1.98 EACH

To win a contest, you must do two of these questions in your head. Which would you choose? Why?

$$\begin{array}{r} 235 \\ + 465 \\ \hline \end{array} \qquad \begin{array}{r} 2000 \\ + 4359 \\ \hline \end{array} \qquad \begin{array}{r} 199 \\ + 199 \\ \hline \end{array}$$

$$\begin{array}{r} 1.50 \\ + 1.50 \\ \hline \end{array}$$

Is the answer reasonable? Why or why not? Write a note to a friend explaining how to find the answer.

$$\begin{array}{r} 1230 \\ - 456 \\ \hline 1226 \end{array}$$

Mona used a calculator to add.

$$\begin{array}{r} 8358 \\ 4509 \\ + 8756 \\ \hline \end{array}$$

She entered 8765 instead of 8756. The display showed 21 632. Tell how Mona can correct her mistake without starting over.

Subtraction models make me mad. So instead of subtracting I always add.

How might Hanif subtract 995 from 1550?

What questions do you still have about addition and subtraction?

Examining

$4.89
for one pack

◄ How many packages are there?
How many batteries are there?
Estimate the total cost.

▼ What is the value of this book
of stamps? of 2 books?
How can you use the value of
this book to find the value of
ten 46¢ stamps?

▼ What is the value of these nickels?

Multiplication

▲ How many bottles do the scouts have?
How much do they get when they return these bottles?

**Special
2 for 89¢**

◄ Will 6 cans of soup cost
more than $2? more than $3?

Find a way to group the students
in your class into equal rows.
Write a multiplication sentence
to describe your grouping.

 How many times is the digit 9 used in the page numbers 1 to 100?

Making Bead-Work Patterns

CROSS SECTION

How many beads are in 2 rows?
3 rows?
How many beads does
Mary Tootoosis need for 4 rows?

You can show your solution in different ways.

$5 + 5 + 5 + 5 = 20$

4 groups of 5 = 20

4 fives = 20

$4 \times 5 = 20$

factors   product

Beautiful and Useful

The Native People of North America use designs with beads to decorate belts, headbands, bags, moccasins, and other clothing.

Most use the overlaid stitch with two needles. One needle holds the beads. The other stitches the bead thread to the buckskin or cloth. The number of beads between the stitches depends on the design.

Model each problem.
Write your solution in different ways.

1. How many beads does Mary need
   for 5 rows?   for 9 rows?

2. Mary has 34 beads.
   Are there enough for 8 rows of 4 beads?
   Are there any left over? If so, how many?

124

3. How many beads are needed to make a pattern for each of these?

$3 + 3 + 3 + 3 + 3 + 3 + 3$

$4 + 4 + 4 + 4 + 4$

$$\begin{array}{r} 5 \\ \times\ 6 \\ \hline \end{array}$$

3×9

8×7

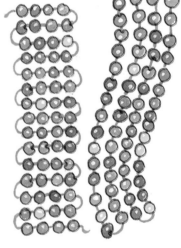

4. How many beads does this pattern use?

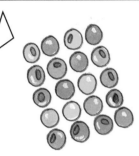

Tell how you can use this pattern to find how many beads are in these patterns.

6×4 $\qquad$ 4×4 $\qquad$ 10×4

5. How can you tell, without counting all of the beads, which bead pattern in each pair uses more beads?

6. How many beads does this pattern use?
Make 2 other patterns that use the same number of beads.

7. Tell how to make different patterns using 24 beads.
Each row should have the same number of beads.

About 4 kg out of every 10 kg of garbage are paper. In 100 kg of garbage, how many kilograms would be saved if the paper was recycled?

Grouping Chairs

Tell how you know there are the same number of chairs in each room.

You can describe this grouping of chairs as

6 rows of 8 = 4 rows of 8 + 2 rows of 8

= 4 eights + 2 eights

= 4 × 8 + 2 × 8

1. Describe this chair grouping with an aisle in different ways.

How many chairs are there altogether?

126

Model your solutions.

2. Find each number of chairs.

   - 4 rows of 9 + 3 rows of 9

   - 6 fives + 3 fives

   - 5 × 4 + 3 × 4

   - 6 × 7 with an aisle in the middle

3. Which groupings have the same number of chairs?

   3 rows of 8 + 4 rows of 8

   1 × 8 + 6 × 8

   2 eights + 6 eights

   7 × 8

4. Show a 6 × 9 chair grouping. How many different groupings, each with 1 aisle, can you make? Describe each grouping.

5. Show an 8 × 8 chair grouping. How many different groupings, each with 2 aisles, can you make? Describe each grouping.

6. How many chairs are there when 1 row is added to each grouping?

   6 rows of 5 = 30

   5 rows of 8 = 40

7. Tell how the first fact can help you find the second.

4 fives = 20	5 rows of 9 = 45	5 × 8 = 40
5 fives = ?	6 rows of 9 = ?	7 × 8 = ?

8. Complete these sentences.

   6 fives = 2 fives + 2 fives + ? fives

   8 rows of 6 = 4 rows of 6 + ? rows of 6

   7 × ? = 6 × ? + 1 × ?

9. Write a multiplication fact you know. Use it to find 2 other facts.

Continue the patterns.

$\frac{1}{2}, \frac{2}{3}, \frac{3}{4}, \boxed{?}, \boxed{?}, \boxed{?},$

$\frac{1}{1}, \frac{2}{2}, \frac{4}{4}, \boxed{?}, \boxed{?}, \boxed{?},$

$1.01, 1.23, 1.45, \boxed{?}, \boxed{?}, \boxed{?},$

Making Rectangles

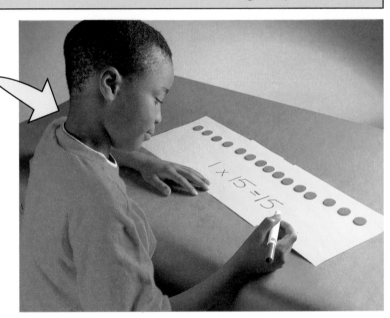

Use 15 counters.
Arrange them into rectangles
in as many ways as you can.

Write a multiplication sentence
for each rectangle.

What do you notice about
all the products? Explain.

Work with a partner.

1. How many different ways can you arrange 12 counters into
   rectangles?
   Write a multiplication sentence for each rectangle.
   Why are there more rectangles using 12 counters than 15 counters?

2. Describe each rectangle with
   a multiplication sentence.
   How are the first factors related?
   the second factors?
   Make the first rectangle.
   Then move two rows to make
   the second one.
   How does this explain the relationships
   between the factors?

3. Make rectangles for each number of counters.
   18 counters   24 counters   30 counters
   Write multiplication sentences. Find pairs of sentences that are related.

128

GROWING RECTANGLES

Draw this rectangle on grid paper.
Double the length and the width.
How many of the first rectangle are needed
to cover the new rectangle?
What if you tripled the length and the width?

NUMBER FAMILY

Which number doesn't belong
in this family? Tell why you think so.
Name another number in the family.

CLUMSY FINGERS

Jiana goofed and multiplied
8×36 instead of 9×36.
How can she find the correct
result without starting over?

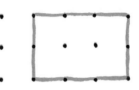

LUCKY LENNY

Lenny is doubly lucky.
On Monday he finds 1 penny.
On Tuesday he finds 2 pennies.
On Wednesday he finds 4 pennies.
On Thursday he finds 8 pennies.
If his luck keeps up, when does he find more than a dollar?

MYSTERY NUMBERS

We are 2 numbers.
If you add us together, our sum is 13.
If you multiply us, our product is 40.
Who are we?

**Make up other problems. Post
them on the bulletin board for
your classmates to solve.**

One side of a rectangle must be 22 cm long.
What rectangle can you make with 50 cm of string?

Shopping at the Craft Store

Multiplying by 10s, 100s, and 1000s

How many rolly eyes would be in
6 packages?

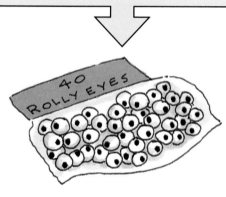

$$\begin{array}{r} 40 \\ 40 \\ 40 \\ 40 \\ 40 \\ + 40 \\ \hline 240 \end{array}$$

6 × 4 tens

$$\begin{array}{r} 40 \\ \times 6 \\ \end{array}$$

4 tens
$$\begin{array}{r} \times 6 \\ \hline 24 \text{ tens} \end{array}$$
or 240

Katie added and Simon multiplied.

How did *you* find how many would
be in 6 packages?

Work with a partner. **Model your solutions.**

1. How many doll pins are there
in 8 packages
of 200?

200 DOLL PINS

2. How many craft sticks are there
in 5 packages
of 80?

80 CRAFT STICKS

3. Use the first multiplication to help you
do the others.

$$\begin{array}{r} 7 \\ \times 8 \\ \hline 56 \end{array} \qquad \begin{array}{r} 70 \\ \times 8 \\ \hline \end{array} \qquad \begin{array}{r} 700 \\ \times 8 \\ \hline \end{array} \qquad \begin{array}{r} 7000 \\ \times 8 \\ \hline \end{array}$$

4. How many more small wooden beads
are there than medium wooden beads?

5. How many packages of 70 pompoms
are needed to have 300 pompoms?

This net folds to make a cube.
Number the sides so that
opposite sides of the cube add to 7.

| | | 6 | 4 |
| | | 2 | |

 aking Frames

Is 150 cm enough to make this frame?

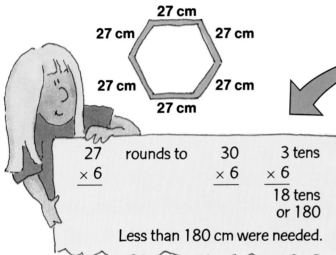

Kaitlyn and Ian estimated. They agreed that 150 cm is not enough.

27	rounds to	30	3 tens
× 6		× 6	× 6
			18 tens or 180

Less than 180 cm were needed.

27
× 6
———
120

6×2 tens $= 12$ tens

Add about 40 more.

About 160 cm were needed.

How does Kaitlyn know that less than 180 cm is needed?

How did Ian know that more than 120 cm is needed?
Why did he add 40 cm?

 **Solve each problem by estimating.**

1. Is 80 cm enough to make this frame? Why or why not?

13 cm   13 cm
13 cm   13 cm
13 cm

2. Is this statement reasonable? Explain.

About 100 cm of framing is enough to make a frame like this.

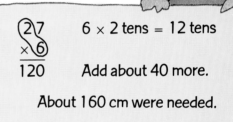
28 cm
28 cm   28 cm
28 cm

3. Which length of framing would you buy to make this frame? Why?

100 cm   150 cm   200 cm

64 cm   64 cm
64 cm

4. Can 2 frames like this be made with 200 cm of framing?

19 cm
19 cm   19 cm
19 cm   19 cm
19 cm

The page number product for this page is
$1 \times 3 \times 2 = 6$
What is the greatest page number product
for this book? the least?

Buying Tickets

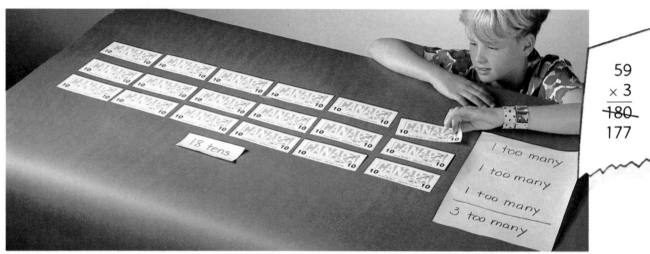

$$\begin{array}{r} 59 \\ \times\ 3 \\ \hline \cancel{180} \\ 177 \end{array}$$

1 too many
1 too many
1 too many
3 too many

18 tens

How is Niki using bills to find the cost of 3 red tickets?
How could she use bills to find the cost of 4 blue tickets?

$27
$37
$48
$59

Work in a group.

Use play money to model your solutions.

Find the cost.

1. 6 blue tickets

2. 4 yellow tickets   **3.** 7 green tickets

4. a red ticket for each member   **5.** 2 red tickets and 2 blue tickets
of your group   Find your answer two ways.

Tell how the first product helps you find the second one.

6.	$80	$78	7.	$200	$199	8.	$90	$87
	× 4	× 4		× 6	× 6		× 7	× 7
	$320			$1200			$630	

9. 6 green tickets cost $162. Use this to find the cost of 6 yellow tickets.

132

MAGIC NUMBERS

Use any number and multiply.
$\boxed{?} \times 5 \times 2 \times 5 \times 2$
Try some other numbers.
How are the products similar? Explain.

BROKEN KEY

How could you find each product on a calculator if the 9 key is broken?

7×59

8×99

6×199

POWERFUL PATTERN

Complete the pattern.
$1 \times 100 + 1 = \boxed{?}$
$2 \times 200 + 2 = \boxed{?}$
$3 \times 300 + 3 = \boxed{?}$
$4 \times 400 + 4 = \boxed{?}$
Predict the next 5 numbers in the pattern.
Check your predictions.

CLOSE TO 200

Find a number to multiply by 7 to get close to 200.
Can you find a number to multiply by 6 to get even closer?
If so, what is it?

PENCIL LINE

A new pencil can draw a line about 60 km long.
Estimate how long a line can be drawn using the pencils in your group.

Make up other problems. Post them on the bulletin board for your classmates to solve.

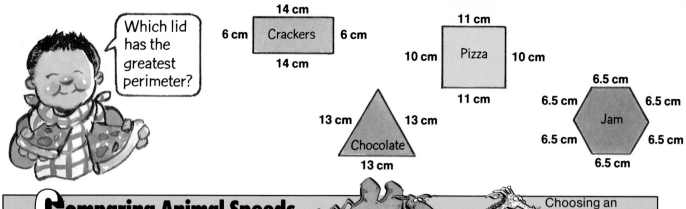

Which lid has the greatest perimeter?

14 cm
6 cm Crackers 6 cm
14 cm

11 cm
10 cm Pizza 10 cm
11 cm

6.5 cm
6.5 cm · 6.5 cm
Jam
6.5 cm · 6.5 cm
6.5 cm

13 cm Chocolate 13 cm
13 cm

Comparing Animal Speeds

Choosing an Algorithm

Estimate how far a greyhound can travel in 4 hours.

Is the actual distance more or less than your estimate? Why?

Distance in 1 Hour

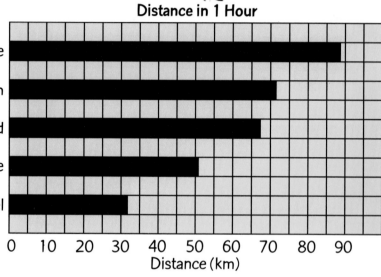

Distance (km)

Ramsay estimated 240 km and then he calculated. Why did he add 28 to his estimate?

1. Estimate and then calculate each distance.
   Model your solutions.
   · antelope in 3 hours
   · ostrich in 5 hours
   · camel in 7 hours

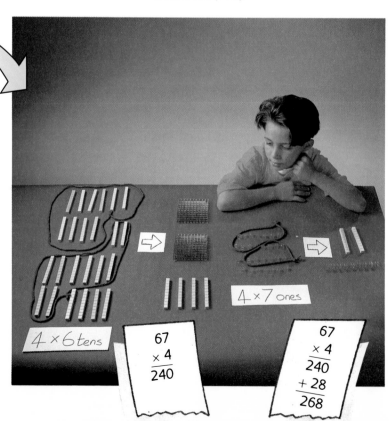

4×6 tens

4×7 ones

$$\begin{array}{r} 67 \\ \times\ 4 \\ \hline 240 \end{array}$$

$$\begin{array}{r} 67 \\ \times\ 4 \\ \hline 240 \\ +\ 28 \\ \hline 268 \end{array}$$

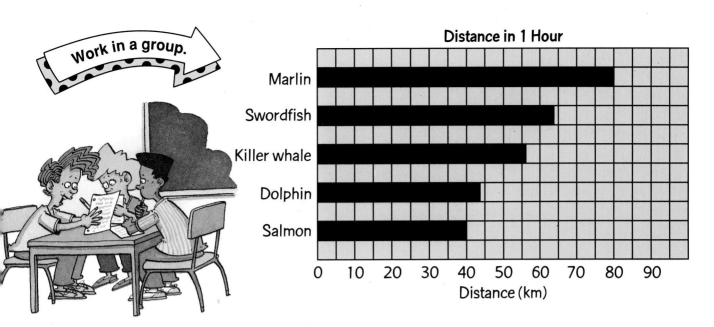

Distance in 1 Hour

	0	10	20	30	40	50	60	70	80	90
Marlin										
Swordfish										
Killer whale										
Dolphin										
Salmon										

Distance (km)

2. Which swimmer travels twice as far as another in the same time? Tell how you decided.

3. Estimate to decide which swimmers travel between 300 km and 500 km in 6 hours.

Calculate each distance. Model your solutions.

4. How far does each swim in 8 hours?

5. How much farther than a killer whale does a swordfish swim in 6 hours?
How can you check your answer using different calculations?

6. How far might each flier travel in 5 hours?
When might they travel these distances?

48 km

61 km

80 km

Distance in 1 hour

7. Make up two multiplying problems about animals for another group to solve.

135

An ant walks 105 cm around the square. At which corner does it stop?

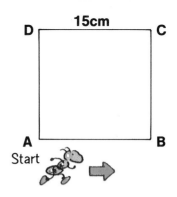

D — 15cm — C

A ___ B

Start

Following Animal Migrations

Choosing an Algorithm

The best food for whales is near the North and South Poles.

But many whales travel to warmer waters when their babies are born.

Blue whales can swim 37 km in an hour.

How far can they travel in 6 hours?

This is how Jeannie found the answer. Explain her work.

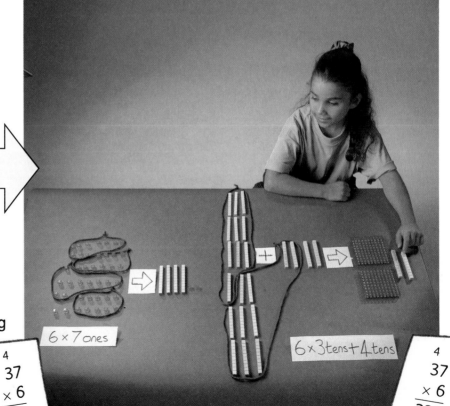

6 × 7 ones

6 × 3 tens + 4 tens

$$\begin{array}{r} 4 \\ 37 \\ \times 6 \\ \hline 2 \end{array}$$

$$\begin{array}{r} 4 \\ 37 \\ \times 6 \\ \hline 222 \end{array}$$

1. Use Jeannie's way to find how far blue whales travel in 8 h. Check your work using another way.

136

Model your solutions.

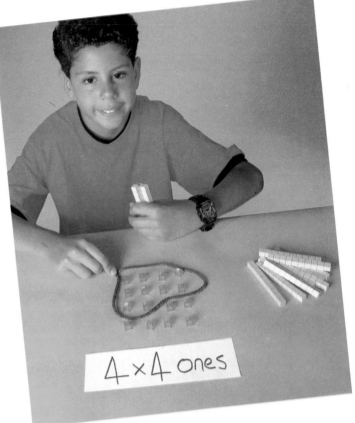

4×4 ones

2. Gray whales can swim only about 4 km in an hour. But they don't sleep when they migrate.

   How far can they swim in 24 hours? in a week?

3. Humpback whales can travel 8 km in an hour.

   How far can they travel in a week? Tell how you found your answer.

   How much farther can humpback whales travel in a week than gray whales?

4. Caribou move from the woods to the tundra in the spring. They can travel about 23 km in a day.

   How far can they travel in a week?

5. Arctic terns can fly 6 km in an hour. How far can they travel in a day?

6. Golden plovers can fly about 8 km in 5 minutes.

   How far can they travel in 1 hour?

137

I am standing in the centre of a container.
My hands can just touch the walls.
Even when I turn, they still touch the walls.
What shape is the container?

Beautifying the Town

225 tulip bulbs were planted in each of 6 beds.

Rosa is calculating how many tulips were planted altogether.

Finish her work.

Check your answer by multiplying another way.

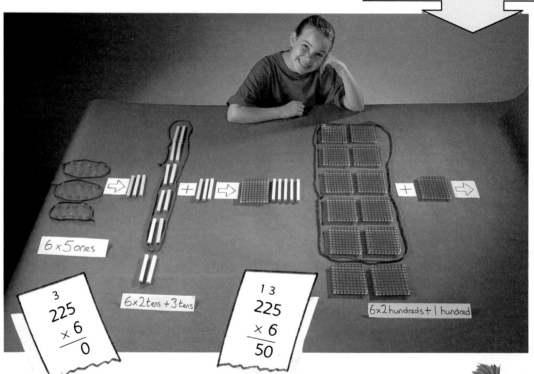

6 × 5 ones

6 × 2 tens + 3 tens

6 × 2 hundreds + 1 hundred

```
  3
 225
 × 6
 ———
   0
```

```
 1 3
 225
 × 6
 ———
  50
```

Work in a group.

Model your solutions.

Check your answers by multiplying another way.

1. 186 daffodil bulbs were planted in each of 4 beds.
   How many were planted altogether?
   How many more would be needed for 6 beds?

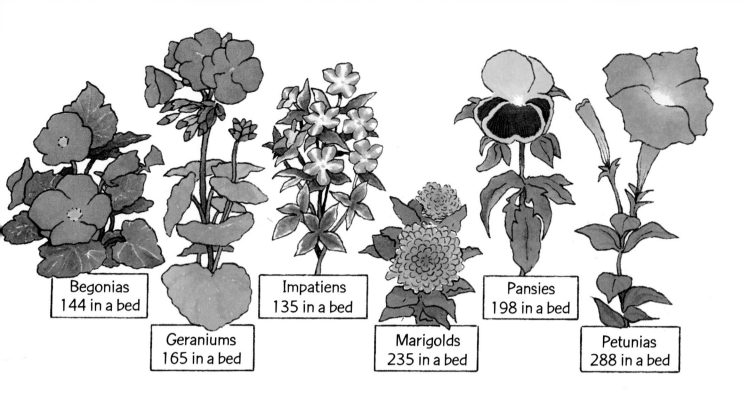

Begonias
144 in a bed

Geraniums
165 in a bed

Impatiens
135 in a bed

Marigolds
235 in a bed

Pansies
198 in a bed

Petunias
288 in a bed

2. There are 8 beds for each plant. Which total do you think would be easiest to find? Why? Try it.

3. Which has more plants? How many more?

| 6 beds of begonias | 4 beds of marigolds |

4. How can finding the number of impatiens in 5 beds help you find the number of marigolds in 5 beds?

5. Find the total number of plants in 3 beds of geraniums and 3 beds of impatiens. Find your answer two ways.

6. How many more plants are in 7 beds of begonias than in 7 beds of impatiens?
Could you answer this in your head?
Explain how.

7. Make up two multiplying problems about beds of plants for another group to solve.

There are lots of ways to calculate 6×73.
Here are some. Can you think of any more?

1. You can use a place value chart.

hundreds	tens	ones

hundreds	tens	ones

$6 \times 73 = 438$

2. You might use doubles and add.

$2 \times 73 = 146$
$4 \times 73 = 292$ double
$6 \times 73 = \overline{438}$

$6 \times 73 = 438$

3. You could estimate and then make it exact.

$$73$$
$$\times\ 6$$
$$\overline{420} \leftarrow \boxed{6 \times 7 \text{ tens}}$$
$$+\ 18 \leftarrow \boxed{6 \times 3}$$
$$\overline{438}$$

$6 \times 73 = 438$

4. You might multiply 6 and 3 ones and then 6 and 7 tens.

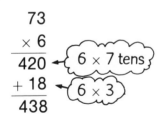

$$\begin{array}{r} 1 \\ 73 \\ \times\ 6 \\ \hline 438 \end{array}$$

$6 \times 73 = 438$

Work in a group.

Show two different ways
to do each multiplication.

1. 9×32 **2.** 7×49

3. $\begin{array}{r} 98 \\ \times\ 6 \end{array}$ **4.** $\begin{array}{r} 56 \\ \times\ 8 \end{array}$ **5.** $\begin{array}{r} 128 \\ \times\ 5 \end{array}$

Take Your Pick

BED TIME

How many hours do you usually sleep each night?
About how many months would it take you to sleep over 1000 hours? over 3000 hours?

A BIG EATER

A meadow mouse has a mass of 25 g. Each day it eats about 50 g of food. About how much would you have to eat in a day to be as big an eater?

WHAT PRICE?

Braedon bought 5 pencils for less than $2.00. What is the most each pencil could have cost?

BLAST FROM THE PAST

Many years ago children multiplied 7 × 57 like this.

$$
\begin{array}{r}
57 \\
\times\ 7 \\
\hline
\end{array}
$$

$$
\begin{array}{rr}
2 \times 57 \rightarrow & 114 \\
2 \times 57 \rightarrow & 114 \\
2 \times 57 \rightarrow & 114 \\
1 \times 57 \rightarrow & 57 \\
\hline
& 399 \\
\end{array}
$$

Use this method to find these products.

3 × 26   5 × 55   7 × 120

MISSING DIGITS

Find the missing digits.

$$
\begin{array}{r}
\boxed{?}\,6\,\boxed{?} \\
\times\quad 4 \\
\hline
2\,0\,0\,0 \\
\boxed{?}\,\boxed{?}\,\boxed{?} \\
+\quad 1\,2 \\
\hline
\boxed{?}\,\boxed{?}\,\boxed{?}\,\boxed{?} \\
\end{array}
$$

Make up other problems. Post them on the bulletin board for your classmates to solve.

Solving a Problem by Finding all the Combinations

Try this problem before going on.

BREAD AND JAM

Eleni is having a slice of bread and jam.
She can have the bread toasted or not.
She can have strawberry, grape, or peach jam.
How many different ways can she have bread and jam?

Mel's group solved the problem by finding all the combinations.

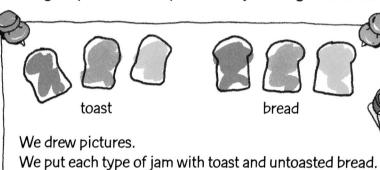

toast   bread

We drew pictures.
We put each type of jam with toast and untoasted bread.
We found 3 types of jam and 2 types of bread gave
6 different ways.

What if Eleni could have another type of jam?

Work in a group.

Solve these problems by finding all the combinations.

ORDERING PIZZA

Pizza sizes are small, medium, and large. The types of pizza are pepperoni, deluxe, supreme, and Hawaiian. Is it possible for 10 customers each to order a different pizza? Explain.

SILLY SENTENCES

Choose one word from each list. How many different sentences can you make?

Red   dogs   jump
Silly   goats   grumble
Wise

SENDING LETTERS

Marnie has white, mauve, and pink envelopes. She has paper in the same colors. She has black, blue, and red ink pens. How many different color combinations are possible for a one-page letter?

Practising What You've Learned

Write a problem for each of these. Then solve.

1. 7×3

2. 5×6

3. $\begin{array}{r} 25 \\ \times\ 9 \\ \hline \end{array}$

4. $\begin{array}{r} 125 \\ \times\ 4 \\ \hline \end{array}$

Solve ONLY the problems where you could use multiplication.

5. What is the cost of mailing this parcel?

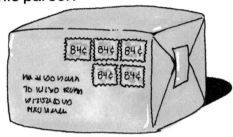

6. What is the cost of this lunch?

7. Ribbon comes in rolls of 175 cm. Adrienne and Greg bought 8 rolls to make awards. How much ribbon did they buy?

8. A 75 kg tennis player lost 3 kg while playing a tough match. How much was his mass after the match?

9. The students hope to sell 858 hot dogs. A package contains 8 wieners. Will 108 packages be enough?

10. How many small juice boxes are needed to have the same amount of juice as in the carton?

125 mL   1 L

11. You want to buy 9 lollipops. What is the least amount of money you need? the greatest amount?

12. Nina built a brick wall 15 bricks high and 8 bricks wide. How many bricks did she use?

143

Play each game in a group of 2, 3, or 4.

Cover Up Products

- Roll two number cubes.
- Find the product of your two numbers on the gameboard.
- Cover the product with a counter.
- Each player uses a different color of counters.
- Take turns until no more counters can be placed.
- The winner is the player with the most counters on the board.

25	30	35	40	45	50
30	36	42	48	54	60
35	42	49	56	63	70
40	48	56	64	72	80
45	54	63	72	81	90
50	60	70	80	90	100

Example   Cover one 50.

Variation: The winner is the first player to place 3 counters in a row.

Use Those Factors

- Shuffle the cards.
- Deal an equal number of cards face down to each player. Set aside the extras.
- Turn over the top card in your pile.
- The player with the greatest product takes all the cards that are face up.
- In case of a tie, the tied players turn over another card.
- Continue until one player has no cards.
- The player with the most cards wins.

Example

5 × 6	4 × 8	3 × 9

takes all 3 cards

Variation: The player with the least product takes all the cards.

Take Your Pick

BLAST FROM THE PAST

This problem is in a math book that is 70 years old.

A man earned $15 a week for 2 weeks and then was out of work for 3 weeks. He paid $4.25 a week for his room and board the whole time. How much of his earnings did he have left?

JUMP!

A jumping mouse can jump 30 times its body length. How far could you jump if you jumped like this mouse?

HOW MUCH WIRE?

Which package uses the greater length of wire? Explain.

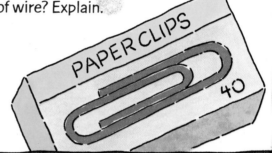

PAPER CLIPS 100

PAPER CLIPS 40

ENJOYING THE JOKE

Jenna makes up a joke and tells it to 2 people on Monday.
Each person who knows the joke tells 3 people on Tuesday.
On Wednesday, each person who knows the joke tells 4 people. How many people know the joke by the end of Wednesday?

FACTOR NINE

Use a calculator to find these products.
What pattern do you notice?
9×1
9×12
9×123
9×1234

Make up other problems. Post them on the bulletin board for your classmates to solve.

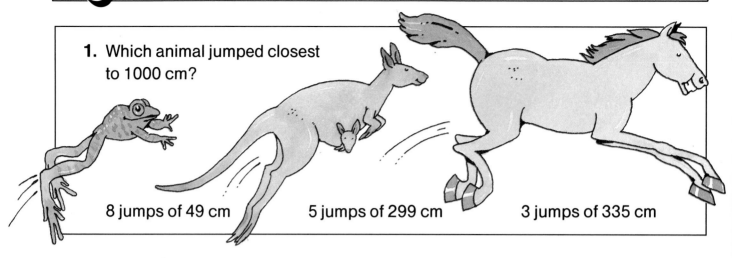

1. Which animal jumped closest to 1000 cm?

8 jumps of 49 cm   5 jumps of 299 cm   3 jumps of 335 cm

2. How does knowing $2 \times 8 = 16$ help you find the product 7×8?

3. How can quarters help you find these products?

8×25 6×25 12×25

4. What is the perimeter of this hexagon?

15 cm
15 cm   15 cm
15 cm   15 cm
15 cm

5. How can you use this table to find the cost of 24 cans of juice?

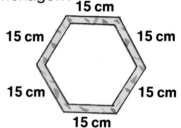

Number of cans	Price ($)
1	0.99
2	1.98
3	2.97

6. What is each missing factor?

$5 \times 25 \times 6 \times \boxed{?} = 0$

$\boxed{?} \times 2 \times 3 \times 5 = 30$

7. If $4 \times 36 < 8 \times \boxed{?}$, what could the missing factor be? Why?

8. Is the product $4 \times \boxed{?}$ even or odd? Tell why you think so.

9. Tell how you know 4×5667 is greater than 20 000.

10. Glenn and Matti's cub troops held a bottle drive. They got 40¢ for each bottle collected. Glenn and Matti each filled 5 cartons. How much money did they bring in?

Is this product less than or greater than 1500?

7 × 257

Explain how you can tell without doing the actual multiplication.

234
× 5
970

Write a note to Mara telling why you knew her answer was wrong before you multiplied.

6 × 7 = 42
4 × 9 = 36
11 × 8 = 88

Write a multiplication fact you know.
Describe how to use it to find other facts.

Explain how you can find these products in your head.

5 × 40

6 × 300

9 × 7000

Why is it easy to order these products from least to greatest without multiplying?

6 × 129   8 × 145   1 × 97

What questions do you still have about multiplication?

Examining

▲ Michelle has saved $40.
How many mugs can she buy for her mother?
How much more money does she need to buy one more mug?
How much does she need to buy 8 mugs?

◄ How could 2 children share fairly 48¢?
$48? $480?
What is the same about the answers?

Division

▲ The teacher decides to arrange 30 desks so that his students can work in groups. How many groups can he make if he puts the desks in groups of 2? groups of 3?

What other ways could he arrange the desks in groups of equal size?

Would it be easy to arrange 31 desks in groups of equal size? Explain.

Describe a situation where you might have to divide a number greater than 100.

COLE SLAW

Use your head. Which of these is closest to 1000?

850 + 100   2450 − 1250   500 + 275

1 + 10 + 100 + 1000   5 × 2 × 5 × 3

Using Markers

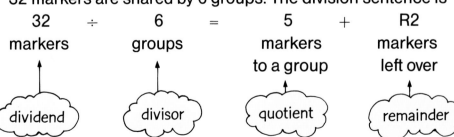

6 groups are making posters.
How many markers are needed for each group to get 2 markers? 3 markers? 4 markers?
How can you use the multiplication table to help you?

×	1	2	3	4	5	6	7	8	9
1	1	2	3	4	5	6	7	8	9
2	2	4	6	8	10	12	14	16	18
3	3	6	9	12	15	18	21	24	27
4	4	8	12	16	20	24	28	32	36
5	5	10	15	20	25	30	35	40	45
6	6	12	18	24	30	36	42	48	54
7	7	14	21	28	35	42	49	56	63
8	8	16	24	32	40	48	56	64	72
9	9	18	27	36	45	54	63	72	81

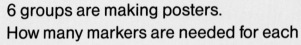

1. Use the table. How many markers does each group get if there are 30 markers? 31 markers?

32 markers are shared by 6 groups. The division sentence is

32	÷	6	=	5	+	R2
markers		groups		markers to a group		markers left over
↑		↑		↑		↑
dividend		divisor		quotient		remainder

2. Write a division sentence for sharing 50 markers among 6 groups. Tell about each number.

Work with a partner.

3. Use the table. How many groups can share 32 markers if 5 markers are given to each group?

Explain the division sentence. Compare it to the division sentence shown on page 150.

4. Explain how each number line shows the number of groups getting markers.
Write each division sentence.

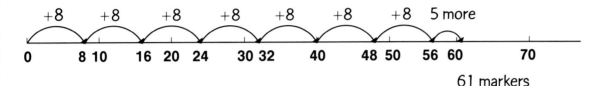

+8   +8   +8   +8   +8   +8   +8   5 more

0   8 10   16 20 24   30 32   40   48 50   56 60   70

61 markers

+6   +6   +6   +6   +6   +6   +6   +6   4 more

0   6   10 12   18 20 24   30   36   40 42   48 50 52   60

52 markers

How is using a number line like using a multiplication table?

Use counters, the multiplication table, or number lines.

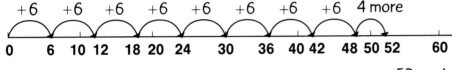

5. How many are left over when each number of markers is shared?
Write the division sentences.

50 → by 5 groups	30 → 7 to a group
60 → by 9 groups	44 → 6 to a group
49 → by 7 groups	38 → 5 to a group

Make up and solve a problem about markers for each division.

6. 37 ÷ 7   **7.** 58 ÷ 9   **8.** 67 ÷ 8   **9.** 0 ÷ 8

Write a note to a friend.

10. Tell which you prefer to use to divide numbers and why.

counters

multiplication table

number line

The school is twice as many blocks from Alice's house as from Fred's. Where could the school be?

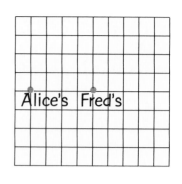

Alice's   Fred's

Sorting Pictures

Relating Division Facts

Toni is sorting family pictures by year.
So far she has   45 for 1989
                 66 for 1990
                 29 for 1991
                 70 for 1992
                 58 for 1993
One album sheet holds 8 pictures.

Toni is using a hundreds chart to find how many sheets she needs for 1989.

1. Why did she mark 48 when there are only 45 pictures?
   How many sheets does she need for 1989?
   Write a division sentence.

2. How many sheets does Toni need for 1990? Write a division sentence.

3. How many sheets does Toni need for each of the other years? Write the division sentences.

4. Toni finds 32 more pictures for 1991. How many sheets does she now need for that year?

5. Toni discovers that 16 of the pictures for 1992 are actually for 1993. How many sheets does she now need for those years?

Is it easier to find the new number of sheets if 20 pictures are moved to 1993? Explain.

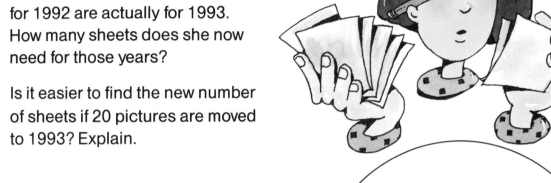

6. Write a problem about pictures for each.

33 ÷ 8

41 ÷ 8

49 ÷ 8

Tell how the answers are related.

7. Write another group of three related divisions. Tell why they are related.

8. The sheets in this album hold 6 pictures. Which number of pictures would use full sheets in this album? in Toni's album?

48   60   65   72   78   80

Which number of pictures would use full sheets in both albums?

Add 8 toothpicks to divide the shape into 4 identical parts that have the same shape as this.

Making Decorations

How many paper doilies are there?

5 are needed for 1 Valentine flower. Estimate how many flowers can be made. Explain your answer.

 12 doilies

12 doilies

12 doilies

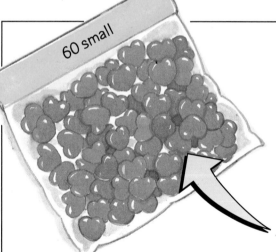 60 small

9 hearts are needed to make 1 centrepiece.

This package of hearts is used.

1. Explain each estimate.

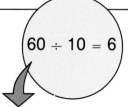 $60 \div 10 = 6$

so there are more than enough to make 6

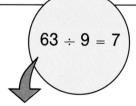 $63 \div 9 = 7$

so there are almost enough to make 7

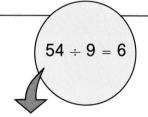 $54 \div 9 = 6$

so there are more than enough to make 6

154

Use facts you know to estimate.

2. 33 ÷ 7 is about ☐   51 ÷ 9 is about ☐   45 ÷ 8 is about ☐

3. Three friends are to make 26 Valentine candy dishes. To share the work fairly, about how many should each make? Suppose they made what you estimated. Would they be a few short or a few over? Explain.

4. The friends are making 8 door knob hearts with ribbons on them.
They have 45 pieces of ribbon.
About how many ribbons are there for each heart? Tell why.

5. They have 6 packages of red hearts.
Each package has 10 hearts.
They need 7 hearts to make one wreath.
About how many wreaths can they make? Tell why.

6. The friends are making 60 Valentine coasters.
They will pack 4 coasters in each box.

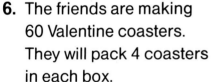

Explain Keifer's thinking.

64 ÷ 8 = 8
We need almost 16 boxes.

Make up and solve a problem about making decorations for each division.

7. 42 ÷ 8 is about ☐

8. ☐ ÷ 7 is about 4

Write a short letter.

9. Tell why estimates are useful.

155

Take Your Pick

PACK THEM UP

32 cookies can be packaged different ways with the same number of cookies in each package.
What are the ways?
Which do you think would be popular to buy?
Why?

ADD THE DIGITS

Find the missing ones digit in each dividend.

$5\boxed{?} \div 9 = 6$ $1\boxed{?} \div 9 = 2$
$2\boxed{?} \div 9 = 3$ $6\boxed{?} \div 9 = 7$
$7\boxed{?} \div 9 = 8$ $3\boxed{?} \div 9 = 4$
$4\boxed{?} \div 9 = 5$ $8\boxed{?} \div 9 = 9$

Add the digits in each dividend.
What do you notice?
Does this apply to divisors other than 9?

THEN TAKE HALF

Jan said that to divide 40 by 8, you divide by 4 and then take half.

$40 \div 8$ $40 \div 4 = 10$ $\frac{1}{2}$ of $10 = 5$

Is this always true for dividing by 8?
Why or why not?
Find a similar way to divide by 6. Explain.

BIG PAILS, SMALL PAILS

$10 is spent on 2 big pails and 1 small one.
A small pail costs half as much as each big one.
How much is spent on a big pail? a small pail?

PUDDING PACKS

Puddings come in packs of 4.
Every school day Sami takes a pudding in his lunch.
How many packs does he need for April?

Make up other problems. Post them on the bulletin board for your classmates to solve.

How can you answer these in your head?

250 + 75   301 − 255   3 × 35

25 × 8 $\frac{1}{2}$ of 240   5 × 17 × 2

Shelving Books

Estimating Larger Quotients

6 students put away 120 library books. How does knowing 12 ÷ 6 help you find each student's share?

What is each share?

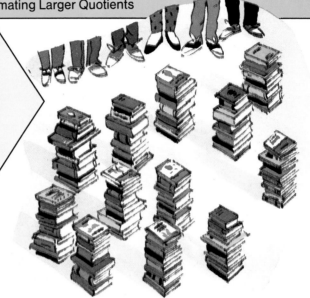

1. 3 students put away 80 library books. Complete this estimate of how many each put away.

80 ÷ 3 is 8 tens ÷ 3
6 tens ÷ 3 = 2 tens
9 tens ÷ 3 = ?
so 8 tens ÷ 3 is about ?

Work in a group.

2. Estimate one student's share if 150 books were put away by

· 4 students   · 5 students   · 6 students

3. 8 students moved 500 library books. Estimate how many each student moved.

4. 6 cartons contained 340 new books. Estimate the number in each carton.

5. 5 students each put away almost 50 books.
About how many books did each carton hold?

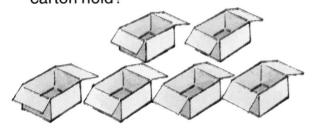

Make up and solve an estimating problem for each division.

6. 110 ÷ 6

7. 130 ÷ 7

157

Deanna ate 100 raisins in 5 days.
Each day she ate 6 more raisins than the day before.
How many raisins did she eat on the first day? the last day?

How would you share 53 marbles among 3?
Ali shared this way.

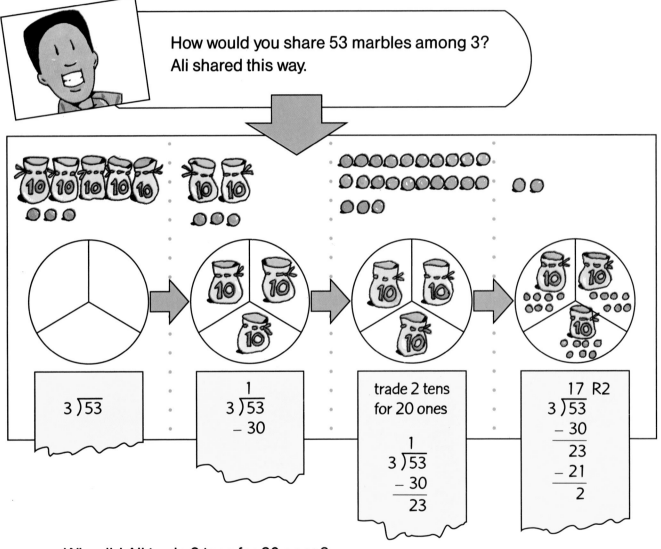

Why did Ali trade 2 tens for 20 ones?

1. Solve Ali's problem using base ten blocks.
What multiplication sentence can be used to check this division?

2. Use base ten blocks to show 90 shared among 7.

158

Use base ten blocks. Check your answers by multiplying.

3. Write each using the $\overline{)}$ sign and show the steps.

$72 \div 5$ $\qquad$ $94 \div 8$

$85 \div 7$ $\qquad$ $80 \div 6$

4. Which of each pair has the greater quotient? Explain.

$55 \div 4$ or $55 \div 5$

$52 \div 6$ or $58 \div 6$

5. Complete so that no trading is needed.

$4\overline{)\boxed{?}\,8}$ $\qquad$ $3\overline{)\boxed{?}\,9}$ $\qquad$ $2\overline{)\boxed{?}\,8}$

Which has the most answers possible for its $\boxed{?}$?

6. Tell how the multiplications can help you do the divisions.

$\begin{array}{r} 18 \\ \times\ 6 \\ \hline 108 \end{array}$	$6\overline{)110}$

$\begin{array}{r} 27 \\ \times\ 4 \\ \hline 108 \end{array}$	$4\overline{)109}$

$\begin{array}{r} 34 \\ \times\ 5 \\ \hline 170 \end{array}$	$5\overline{)173}$

Make up and solve a problem about sharing marbles for each division.

7. $38 \div 3$ $\qquad\qquad$ **8.** $94 \div 2$

9. $56 \div 6$ $\qquad\qquad$ **10.** 2 marbles are left over

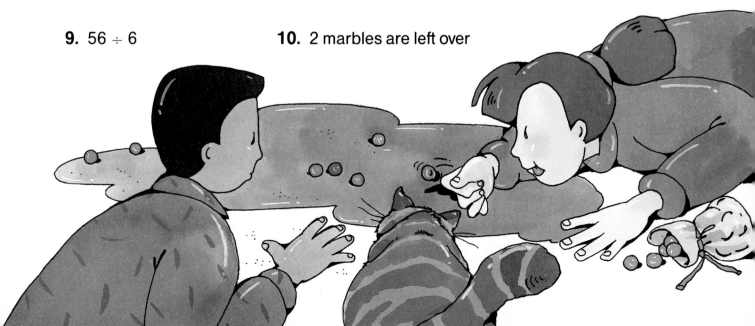

About how much is a square of dimes 36 cm on each side worth?

Packing Pop Bottles

Choosing an Algorithm

A carton holds 6 bottles.
How many cartons are needed
for 86 bottles?

Shina used a number line
to solve the problem.

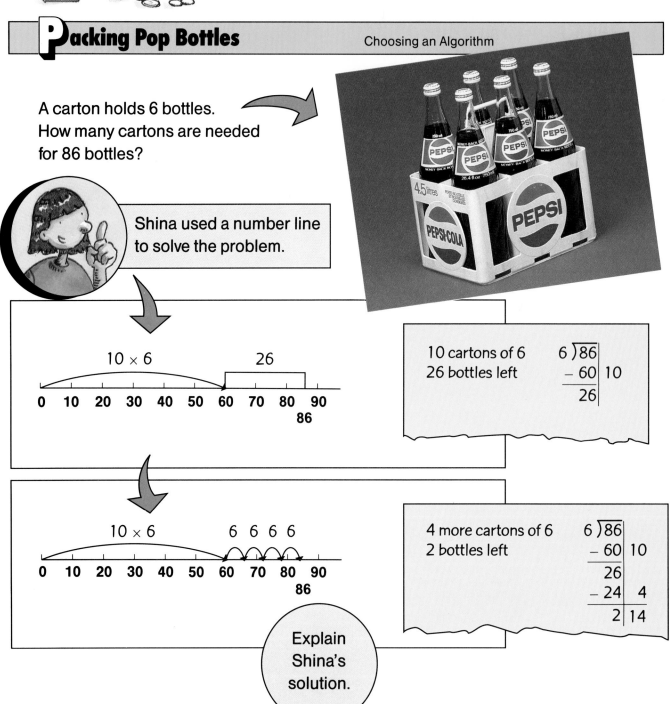

10 × 6   26

0 10 20 30 40 50 60 70 80 90
86

10 cartons of 6   6)86
26 bottles left   − 60 | 10
26

10 × 6   6 6 6 6

0 10 20 30 40 50 60 70 80 90
86

4 more cartons of 6   6)86
2 bottles left   − 60 | 10
26
− 24 | 4
2 | 14

Explain
Shina's
solution.

1. Use a number line to show how many cartons are needed for
   • 96 bottles   • 130 bottles   • 145 bottles

2. What division is shown by each number line?

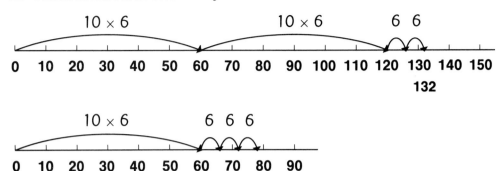

10 × 6   10 × 6   6 6

0 10 20 30 40 50 60 70 80 90 100 110 120 130 140 150

132

10 × 6   6 6 6

0 10 20 30 40 50 60 70 80 90

78

3. What division does each check?

13	20
× 6	× 6
78	120
+ 1	+ 5
79	125

Use a number line.

Use the)‾‾‾ **sign and show the steps.**

Check your answers by multiplying.

4. Gary packed 75 pop bottles. Kim packed 61. Leo packed 50.
How many full cartons did each boy have?
Is there enough for another carton using the left-over bottles? Explain.

5. A company makes cartons that hold 5 bottles.
How many cartons are needed for 60 bottles? 72 bottles? 80 bottles?

6. Another company makes cartons that hold 8 bottles.
How many bottles can be packed in either the 6-bottle cartons or the 8-bottle cartons without any left over?

7. Which size of carton do you think is best? Why?

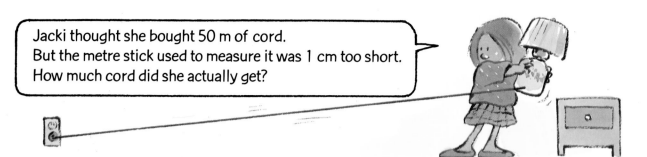

Jacki thought she bought 50 m of cord.
But the metre stick used to measure it was 1 cm too short.
How much cord did she actually get?

D onating to Charity

Extending an Algorithm

Jay's school raised $660 to donate to 5 charities.
How would you share this money fairly?
Jay used play money to model a solution.

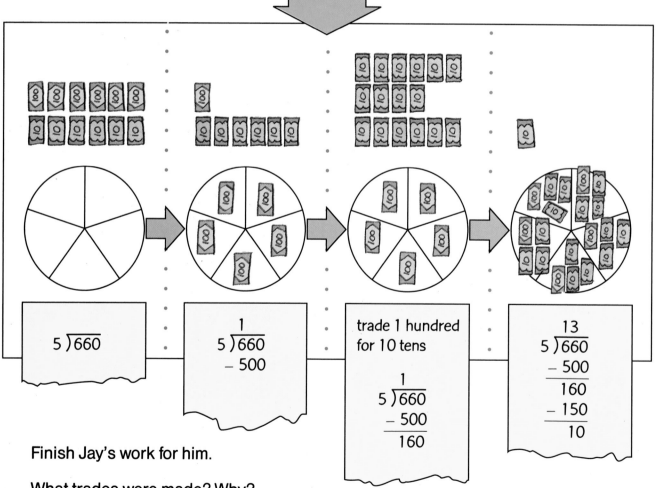

$$5 \overline{)660}$$

$$\begin{array}{r} 1 \\ 5 \overline{)660} \\ -500 \end{array}$$

trade 1 hundred for 10 tens

$$\begin{array}{r} 1 \\ 5 \overline{)660} \\ -500 \\ \hline 160 \end{array}$$

$$\begin{array}{r} 13 \\ 5 \overline{)660} \\ -500 \\ \hline 160 \\ -150 \\ \hline 10 \end{array}$$

Finish Jay's work for him.

What trades were made? Why?

What multiplication sentence can be used to check this division?

1. Show how to share $363 among 3 charities.
Did you need to trade? Check by multiplying.

162

Use play money or base ten blocks.
Check by multiplying.

2. Write each sharing using
   the $\overline{)}$ sign
   and show the steps.

   $435 among 3 charities
   $234 among 6 charities
   $425 among 5 charities
   $432 among 4 charities

3. Show $462 shared among
   8 charities.
   How is this sharing different from
   those above?

4. Complete so that no trading is needed.

   $2\overline{)4\boxed{?}8}$ $3\overline{)\boxed{?}93}$ $4\overline{)\boxed{?}44}$

   Which had the most answers possible for its $\boxed{?}$?

5. Is trading necessary in this division? Explain.

   $5\overline{)4\boxed{?}\boxed{?}}$

6. A school raised $450 to donate to charities.
   Each charity received the same amount.
   Each received at least $100.
   How many charities could there
   have been?

7. Make up 2 money sharing problems
   where the shares are about $200.
   How did you choose your numbers?

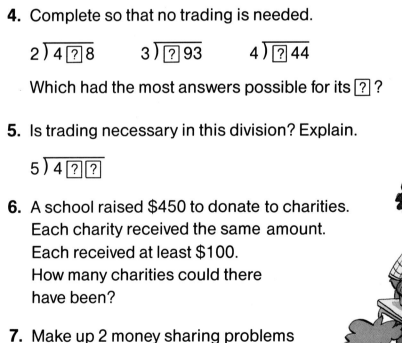

Collecting Bread Tags

Finding Averages

Wayne and Audrey collected
these bread tags.

How could you split them fairly between the two students?
How does 36 ÷ 2 describe this splitting?
We say the average number of bread tags collected by the students is 18.

1. Use different ways to find the average number of bread tags
collected by these students.

   Yanni 18   Shane 24   Nicole 23

Work in a group.

2. How could you decide if 2, 12, and 22
have the same average as 3, 12, and 21
without calculating the average?

3. Why is it easy to find the average
of 2, 2, 2, and 2?
of 23 and 25?

4. If the average number of bread tags that 3 students collected was
22, could one student actually have collected 22? Explain.

Dividing

There are lots of ways to calculate 175 ÷ 8.
Here are some. Can you think of any more?

---

1. You might use base ten blocks and share among 8.

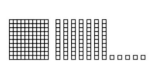

$175 \div 8 = 21 + R7$

---

2. You could use square grids and make groups of 8.

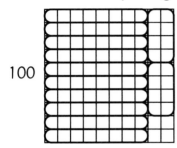

100

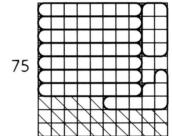

75

21 groups
and 7 left

$175 \div 8 = 21 + R7$

---

3. You could use a number line.

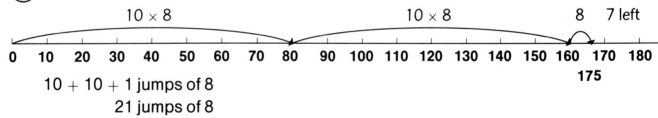

10×8 ⟶ 10×8 ⟶ 8   7 left

0 10 20 30 40 50 60 70 80 90 100 110 120 130 140 150 160 170 180

175

10 + 10 + 1 jumps of 8
21 jumps of 8
and 7 left

$175 \div 8 = 21 + R7$

---

4. You might consider 175 as the sum
of numbers that are easy to divide
by 8.

$175 = 80 + 80 + 15$
$80 \div 8 = 10$
$80 \div 8 = 10$
$15 \div 8 = \underline{1 + R7}$
$21 + R7$ $175 \div 8 = 21 + R7$

 **Work in a group.**

Show two
different ways
to do each
division.

1. $5 \overline{)84}$

2. $9 \overline{)125}$ **3.** $7 \overline{)100}$

4. $93 \div 6$ **5.** $78 \div 4$

FOUR NUMBERS

100, 101, 102, and 103 are consecutive numbers.
Which of them can be divided evenly by 4?
Can you find four consecutive numbers where
none of them can be divided by 4? Explain.

ONLY ONCE

Use any of these cards.

Arrange them to make the following true.

GRANDMOTHER'S GIFT

A grandmother gave each of her 4 grandchildren an equal share of money.
She gave 4 $100 bills, some $10 bills, and some $1 coins.
Each grandchild received more $10 bills than $100 bills,
and more $1 coins than $10 bills.
What is the least amount she could have given away?

AVERAGE SENTENCE

Find a way to estimate the
average number of words
in a sentence in your
favorite story book.
What is your estimate?

CALCULATOR KEYS

Use only the keys [2], [3], [4], [÷], and [=].
You can use each key as often as you like.
Make the display show 78.
Record your solution.

**Make up other problems. Post them
on the bulletin board for your
classmates to solve.**

Solving a Problem by Guessing and Checking

Try this problem before going on.

THE NUMBERS ARE . . . ?

A 1-digit number and a 2-digit number have a sum of 90 and a quotient of 14.
What are the numbers?

Jalisa's group solved the problem by guessing and checking.

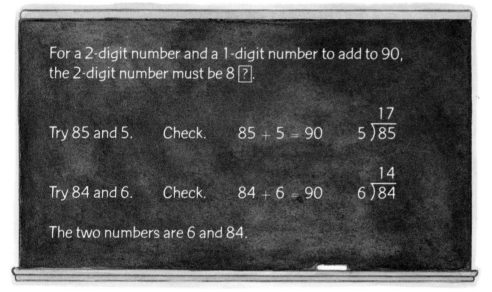

For a 2-digit number and a 1-digit number to add to 90, the 2-digit number must be 8 [?].

Try 85 and 5.   Check.   85 + 5 = 90   5)85
                                                    17

Try 84 and 6.   Check.   84 + 6 = 90   6)84
                                                    14

The two numbers are 6 and 84.

Make up a similar problem for others to solve.

Work in a group.

Solve each problem by guessing and checking.

MOSTLY ODD

Use odd digits for all but one to make this true.

[?][?][?]
[?])[?][?][?]

Can you find other answers?

CUTTING WOOD

If a piece of wood is cut into 3 cm pieces, 1 cm is left. If it's cut into 4 cm pieces, or 5 cm pieces, 1 cm is still left. How long is the original piece of wood?

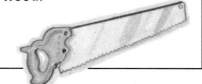

DOUBLE DIVIDE

A number is divided by 3. The remainder is 1. When the quotient is divided by 5, the remainder is 2.
What could the original number be?

Practising What You've Learned

Write a problem for each of these. Then solve.

1. $107 \div 9$

2. the average of 35 and 69

3. $\frac{1}{6}$ of 78

4. $93 \div 4$

5.

Solve ONLY the problems where you could use division.

6. Jenny has 82¢.
What is the greatest number of nickels she could have?

7. Rick ordered 53 cartons of 6 bottles of pop.
How many bottles did he order?

8. Alyson drove 278 km in 3 hours.
Estimate the average distance she drove each hour.

9. Gina cut 8 cm pieces from 290 cm of ribbon.
How many 8 cm pieces did she get?
How much was left?

10. A square has a perimeter of 40 cm.
What is the length of each side?

11. Kalil said it was 81 days until the summer vacation.
How many full weeks is that?

12. Eight sundaes can be made from one carton of ice cream.
How many sundaes can be made from 24 cartons?

168

Playing Games for Practice

Play each game in a group of 2, 3, or 4.

Scoring Ones

- Shuffle the cards. Place them face down in a pile.
- Roll a die and turn over that number of cards.
- Find the average of the numbers on the cards.
- Take turns. The ones digit in the quotient is the number of spaces you move on the gameboard.

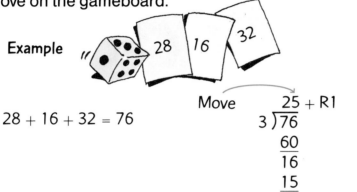

Example

28 16 32

$28 + 16 + 32 = 76$

Move

$$\begin{array}{r} 25 + R1 \\ 3\overline{)76} \\ 60 \\ \hline 16 \\ 15 \\ \hline 1 \end{array}$$

Twenty Plus

- Roll one die twice to create a 2-digit dividend.
- Roll again to get a 1-digit divisor.
- Divide. Your score is 1 if the remainder is 0,
  - 2 if the quotient is 20 or greater,
  - 3 if both of the above are true.
- Take turns. The first player to reach 10 points wins.

Example

 Either 26 or 62 is the dividend.

 3 is the divisor.

If you choose 26, $26 \div 3 = 8 + R2$ Score 0.

If you choose 62, $62 \div 3 = 20 + R2$ Score 2.

Variations:
- Roll one die 3 times to create a 3-digit dividend.
- Use a number cube with 4, 5, 6, 7, 8, and 9 on it.

FAST READERS

Susie usually reads 200 words a minute.
She wrote a story that took her 5 min to read.
If she could read her story in 1 min less,
how many words a minute could she read?

  ## AVERAGE OF FOUR

The average of 10, 20, 21, and 22 is greater than one of them.
The average of 10, 11, 20, and 21 is greater than two of them.
Find four numbers whose average is greater than three of them.

PATTERN OF FOURS

Find all possible remainders when numbers ending in 4 are divided by 4.
What pattern did you find? Explain.

FILL THE BLANKS

Complete to make this true.

```
       1 ? ?
   ? ) 6 ? ?
     ? 0 0
     2 ? ?
     2 0 0
       ? ?
       1 2
        3
```

WHAT COINS?

Franny has 50 coins worth between $5 and $6.
What coins might she have?
How many different answers did your class find?

**Make up other problems. Post
them on the bulletin board for
your classmates to solve.**

1. Make up and solve a problem about sharing for 382 ÷ 4.

2. Are there any hundreds in the quotient for 3)‾258‾ ? Explain.

3. Estimate. Then calculate.

   49 ÷ 8   425 ÷ 6   610 ÷ 7

4. What digits could you use for ☐ in 4)‾☐ 32‾ so that the quotient has 2 digits? 3 digits?

5. What is the greatest remainder you can get when you divide by 8?

6. How does knowing 88 ÷ 2 help you to find 88 ÷ 4?

7. If you divide a 3-digit number by a 1-digit number, what is the lowest quotient possible? the greatest quotient possible?

8. A hockey team plays 80 games. Each game has 3 regular periods. They play 10 overtime periods. How many periods does the team play?

9. Order these from greatest to least without calculating.

   84 × 4   84 ÷ 4   162 × 4   162 ÷ 4

10. A square, an equilateral triangle, and a pentagon have all sides equal. Each has a perimeter of 60 cm. Which shape has the longest sides? Why?

 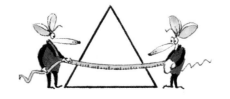 

Ray wants to know whether to divide 140 by 7 in his head or use paper and pencil? What advice would you give him?

Explain how you would use multiplication to check this.

$$5{\overline{\smash{\big)}\,177}}\ \ 35 + R2$$

The average mass of a 10-year-old is about 32 kg.
Explain what this means.
How might you check this?

What would you include in a poster to show what division is all about?

How would you explain to a friend how to correct this error?

$$5{\overline{\smash{\big)}\,515}}\ \ 13$$

DIVISION ?

What questions do you still have about division?

172

Investigating Personal Bests

What activities are you good at? Which do you do the best?
How could numbers show if you are good?
Does a higher number always mean a better performance?
Do you think it is more important to be good at something or to have
fun doing it? Why?

HOW Far Can We Fly Our Flying Machines?

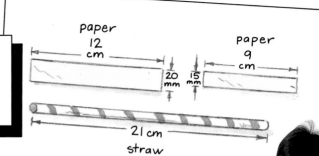

paper 12 cm

paper 9 cm

20 mm   15 mm

21 cm straw

1. Do you think you would be better at creating or flying these flying machines? Why?

FLYING WONDER

Work in a group.

2. Build 10 flying machines by taping strips of paper onto straws. Make each one different.

3. Name each flying machine. Predict which will fly
• the greatest distance
• the least distance

MAGIC FLYER

4. Mark a starting line.
Fly each flying machine 3 times.
Estimate the distance in centimetres from the start to where each one lands. Then measure.
Record the distances in a table. Compare them.
Were your predictions right?

Flying Machine	Distances in Centimetres					
	First flight		Second flight		Third flight	
	Est.	Meas.	Est.	Meas.	Est.	Meas.
Flying Wonder	100	68	200	254	200	195
Magic Flyer						
Smooth Gliding						
My Machine						

5. Draw a bar graph to show the greatest distance of each flying machine. Use one square to represent 10 cm. Record the distance for each machine showing hundredths of a metre.

6. Exchange your flying machines, table, and graph with another group. Choose which of the other group's flying machines is the best. Give your reasons.

7. Combine your flying machines with the other group's. Find the average distance for each machine. Order them from least to greatest average distance. Use your results to tell how to build a better flying machine.

Did you Know...?

Otto Lilienthal was the first person to pilot a glider. From 1891 to 1896, he built about 7 gliders. His farthest flight was about 350 m.

▶ About how far is 350 m from your starting line? About how many times would you have to fly your best flying machine to cover this distance?

How Many Can We Score?

In a round of pailball, each player has 5 tosses.
The score is written as a fraction with fifths.

1. Do you think you would be good at pailball?
   Why or why not?

2. What is the fewest number of goals possible for a round?
   What fraction shows a score you think is likely for you?
   unlikely for you?

3. Decide how far to stand from the pail.
   Take turns for a round of 5 tosses.
   What fraction of the 5 tosses did you score?

4. If you throw from farther back, will your chances be better or worse?
   Why?
   Try longer distances for rounds of 5 tosses.
   What fraction did you score for your best distance?

5. Experiment with the pail at different angles.
   What fraction did you score for your best angle?
   What position of the pail would make it impossible to score a goal?

176

6. Do you think your chances will be better or worse with fancy shots? Why?
   Experiment with a few rounds of 5 fancy shots.
   What fraction did you score with your best fancy shot?

7. Mark the fractions for your best distance, angle, and fancy shot on three number lines.

Best Fancy Shot

$$\frac{0}{5} \quad \frac{1}{5} \quad \frac{2}{5} \quad \frac{3}{5} \quad \frac{4}{5} \quad \frac{5}{5}$$

8. Try rounds of 10 tosses using the same distance, angle, and fancy shot.
   Tally your scores and mark these fractions on number lines.
   Use your number lines to compare the fractions for 10 tosses with the fractions for 5 tosses. Which is your best?

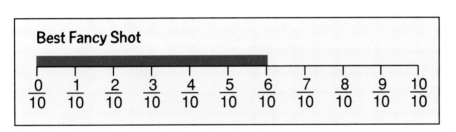

Best Fancy Shot

$$\frac{0}{10} \quad \frac{1}{10} \quad \frac{2}{10} \quad \frac{3}{10} \quad \frac{4}{10} \quad \frac{5}{10} \quad \frac{6}{10} \quad \frac{7}{10} \quad \frac{8}{10} \quad \frac{9}{10} \quad \frac{10}{10}$$

9. Explain your six number lines to your group.
   Tell how you know which is your best kind of toss.
   Is it the same as the toss with your best score?

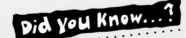

Did you Know...?

The Canadian basketball team won a silver medal in the 1936 Olympics in Berlin. They won their first game against Brazil with a score of 24 to 17. They scored a total of 179 points in the 6 games they played.

▶ What was the average number of points they scored in a game?
   What was the average in the last 5 games?

177

HOW Fast Can We Do Puzzles?

A tangram is a square divided into these 7 pieces. The pieces can be put together in different ways as puzzles.

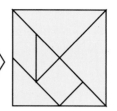

1. Do you think you would be good at solving tangram puzzles? at creating them? Why or why not?

2. Cut out the 7 tangram pieces.

Work with a partner.

3. Choose a puzzle. Use all 7 pieces. Record your starting time. When you finish the puzzle or decide to stop, record the time. Calculate how fast you did each puzzle. Try this with at least 5 tangram puzzles.

Puzzle: E
Finish 3:12
Start 2:55

5 + 12 = 17
17 min for Puzzle E

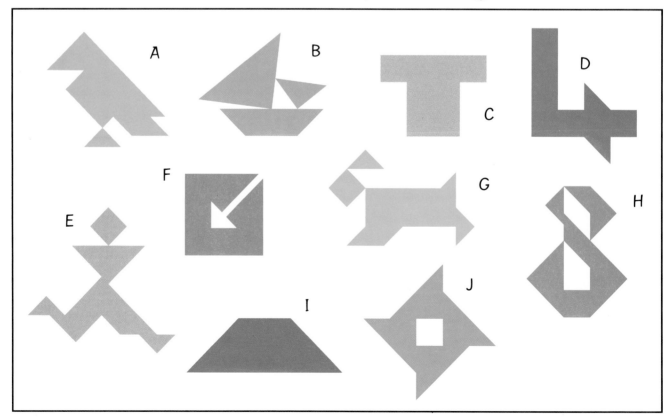

A   B   C   D   F   G   H   E   I   J

4. Draw a bar graph for your 5 best times.
   Find the average.
   Compare the average with the other times.
   Draw a line on the graph to show the average.
   How many minutes altogether do the bars reach
   beyond the line? fall short of the line?

5. Show your graph to other pairs.
   Invite them to ask you questions
   about it.

6. Create some tangram puzzles
   for other pairs to try.

Did you Know...?

Computers like this can be programmed to do about
1000 multiplication or division questions in a second.

▶ Ask someone to time how long it takes you to do some
multiplication questions. Use the results to estimate
how long it would take you to do 1000 multiplication
questions.

? I Wonder... ?

Does Age Matter?

Can 10-year-olds count to 100 faster than 9-year-olds?
Can 10-year-olds count by 10s to 1000 faster than 9-year-olds?

Different Bests

Are the fastest runners the best basketball shooters?

Trying Different Ways

How many pattern blocks can you use for a tower without it collapsing?
What if different building materials are used?
What is the best way to build a tower?
How do you know which tower is best?

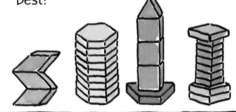

Throwing a Badminton Bird

Can you throw a badminton bird farther than you can hit it with a racket?

Best Circle

Who can draw the best circle using their writing hand? their other hand? with eyes closed?

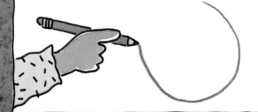

Make up your OWN investigation. Then post it on the bulletin board for others to try.

Thinking Back

Tell how you could find out who is the best juggler. Could numbers be used to find out?

Name 4 books that you like. How could you decide which book you like best? How could you decide which book your classmates like best?

Write about something you do well that is difficult to measure.

How do you know you are good at it?

How can you find out if someone else is good at it?

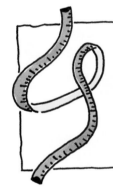

Racer	Race	Time
Manuel	100 m dash	15.9 s
Jordi	150 m obstacle	36.3 s
Theresa	20 m sand spoon	10.8 s
Shani	400 m distance	82.7 s

Who do you think would win a 200 m walking race? Why?
Who do you think would win a 45 m hopping race? Why?

What else would you like to know about personal bests? Tell what you would do to find out.

Exploring

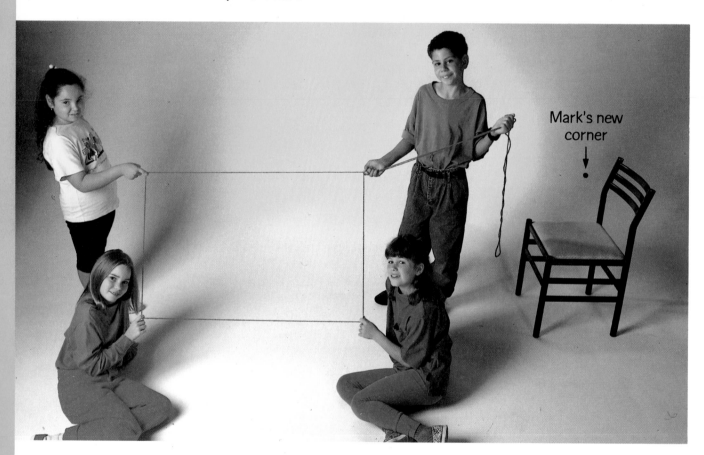

▼ Describe the shape created by the string.
Suppose the string is long enough for Mark to move to the chair.
Describe the shape created.

Mark's new corner

Use a loop of string to create each shape.
Draw a diagram of each.
- 4 sides all the same length and square corners
- 4 sides all different lengths
- 4 sides all the same length and no square corners
- 4 sides of a kite

Quadrilaterals

◄ What 4-sided shapes do you see that are like your diagrams?
Are there any other 4-sided shapes?
Where are they?

Look around your classroom.
What do you see that is square?
Describe a square.

What do you see that is rectangular?
Describe a rectangle.
Do you see more squares or other rectangles? Why do you think that is?

183

What is the change from a dollar for each purchase?
The prices include tax.

68¢   87¢   79¢   72¢   94¢

What is the total change?

Flying Flags

History of Flags

The first known flags were used by Ancient Egyptians. They were streamers on the tops of long poles.
The flags of most countries are rectangles.
Storm warning flags are trapezoids.

All shapes with 4 sides are called quadrilaterals.
Squares and rectangles are two special types of quadrilaterals.
Can you find an example of each in the flags?

Canada

Brazil

Jordan

Manitoba

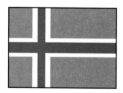

Norway

Arkansas

Maryland

Delaware

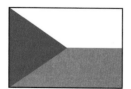

Czechoslovakia

Trinidad and Tobago

Kuwait

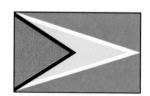

Guyana

Northwest Territories

St. Vincent and the Grenadines

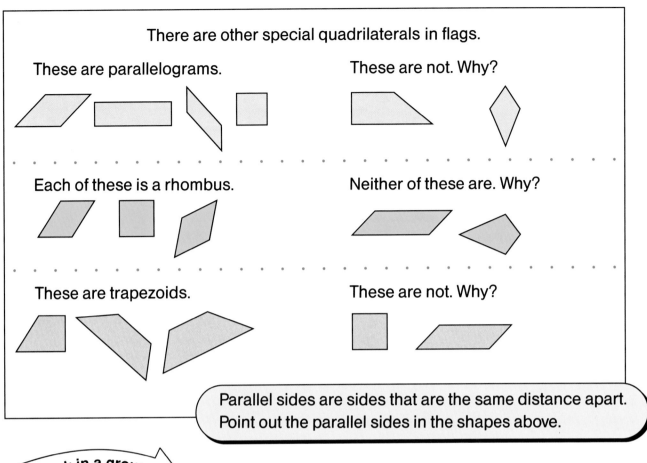

There are other special quadrilaterals in flags.

These are parallelograms.

These are not. Why?

Each of these is a rhombus.

Neither of these are. Why?

These are trapezoids.

These are not. Why?

Parallel sides are sides that are the same distance apart.
Point out the parallel sides in the shapes above.

Work in a group.

Use the flags.

1. Identify each quadrilateral in each flag using the best name.
   Tell how many there are of each type.
   Use a chart like this. Canada's flag is done for you.

	Type of Quadrilateral					
	Square	Rectangle	Parallelogram	Rhombus	Trapezoid	Other
Canada	1	2	–	–	–	–
Brazil	?	?	?	?	?	
Jordan	?	?	?			

2. Which flags have more than one
   type of quadrilateral?

3. Which flag has the most types
   of quadrilaterals?

4. Which flag has the most
   quadrilaterals?

5. Design a flag that contains at least
   3 different types of quadrilaterals.

185

Make a pattern like this for 5 additions.

Roll a die 10 times.
Each time you roll, record the number in one of your spaces.
Try to get as many even sums as possible.

F itting Screens

Exploring Properties of Quadrilaterals

How many ways can Sofi fit the screen into her tent? To find out, try this.

I think this will fit lots of different ways.

Trace and cut out this square.

Save the paper with the hole.

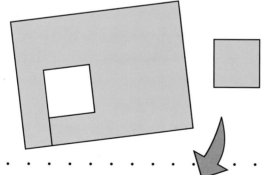

Number the corners like this.

1	2
4	3

Front

5	6
8	7

Back

How many ways does this square fit into its hole?

186

1. Use the method you used for the square screen. How many ways will each screen fit its opening?

2. How many ways will a rhombus screen fit its opening? Explain. Could the answer be different for different-sized rhombuses? Explain.

3. Design a quadrilateral screen that will fit its opening only one way. How is this quadrilateral different from the others you examined?

4. Can you design a quadrilateral screen that will fit its opening exactly 3 ways? Explain.

5. Why are there more ways to fit some quadrilateral screens than others?

DIAGONAL CUT

A square can be cut along a diagonal into 2 triangles with the same size and shape.
What other quadrilaterals can be cut along a diagonal into 2 triangles that are the same?

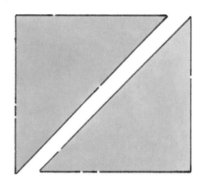

MIRROR, MIRROR

A mirror placed on this card

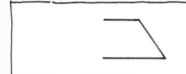

makes a trapezoid.

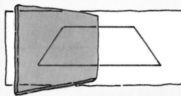

Make 3 other cards that you can place a mirror on to make the same trapezoid.

SPLITTING QUADRILATERALS

A trapezoid can be split into 3 trapezoids.

What other quadrilaterals can be split into 3 of the same type of quadrilateral? 4 of the same type? Which can't?

CANADIAN CITIES

Look at a map of Canada.
Find four cities that could be the corners of
• a parallelogram
• a trapezoid

PARALLELOGRAMS

How many parallelograms that are not squares or rectangles can you make using 9 dots?

Make up other problems. Post them on the bulletin board for your classmates to solve.

Arrange 13 toothpicks to make four squares all the same size. Remove one toothpick so that three squares remain.

Breaking up Squares

Divide a square into four pieces by folding and then cutting from corner to corner.
Arrange the four pieces to make different shapes.

Work with a partner.

1. Use all four pieces to make
   - a rectangle
   - a parallelogram
   - a trapezoid

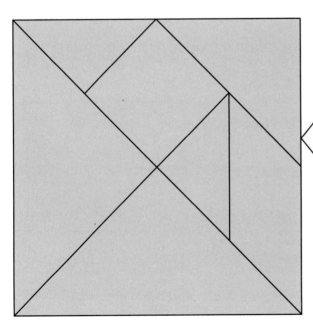

2. Some of the seven tangram pieces are quadrilaterals.
   Which quadrilaterals are they?

3. Use two tangram pieces to make
   - a square
   - a parallelogram
   - a trapezoid

4. Use more than two tangram pieces to make
   - a square
   - a rectangle
   - a parallelogram
   - a trapezoid

5. Create a square puzzle with four pieces for other pairs to solve.
   At least two pieces should be quadrilaterals.

189

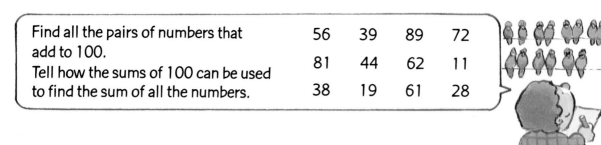

Find all the pairs of numbers that add to 100.
Tell how the sums of 100 can be used to find the sum of all the numbers.

56	39	89	72
81	44	62	11
38	19	61	28

Using Nets

Making Geometric Solids

Nets can be used to make solid shapes.

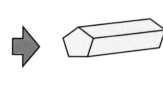

Work in a group.

1. Use nets to make these solid shapes.

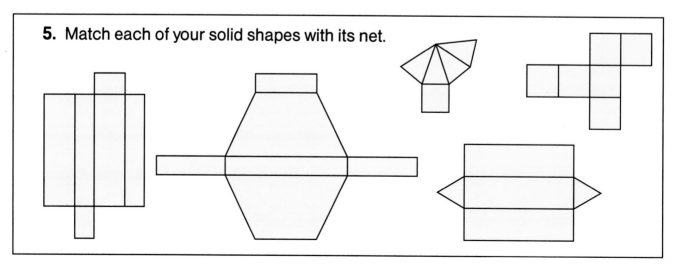

Use your models.

2. Which one is not a prism? Explain.

3. What types of quadrilaterals are the faces? Which type is most common?

4. Which prisms have the same number of faces? Why?

5. Match each of your solid shapes with its net.

6. How many edges and corners does your cube have?
Would you prefer to use a solid shape or its net to count its edges and corners? Why?

190

MAKING BOXES

5 squares form the net of this open box.

How can you cut a sheet of squares like this to make 4 nets for open boxes?

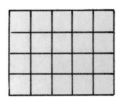

FOLD IT UP

Can this net be folded into a solid shape? Explain.

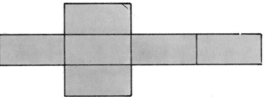

RECTANGLE TO PARALLELOGRAM

Which type of quadrilateral are the faces of this prism?

How could you slice this solid to make parallelogram faces?

USE TWO

What shapes can you make using two rhombuses? two trapezoids?

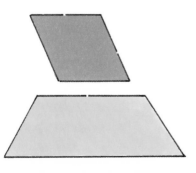

TWO INTO ONE

When can you put together 2 rectangles to make a larger rectangle? 2 squares to make a larger square? Does this work for all types of quadrilaterals? Which ones?

Make up other problems. Post them on the bulletin board for your classmates to solve.

With only an 8 L pail, a 3 L pail, and a barrel of water, how could you fill the 3 L pail $\frac{1}{3}$ full? the 3 L pail $\frac{2}{3}$ full? the 8 L pail $\frac{1}{2}$ full?

Making Ornaments

These ornaments are to be finished by having ribbon glued around them.

How much ribbon is needed for this ornament?
What is the distance around a shape called?

Work in a group.

1. What type of quadrilateral is each ornament?
   Estimate which has
   • the greatest perimeter
   • the least

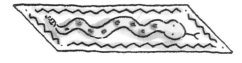

2. Measure and then calculate each perimeter. Check your estimates.

192

3. Trace this ornament.

Draw a trapezoid with a greater perimeter.

Draw a parallelogram with a lesser perimeter.

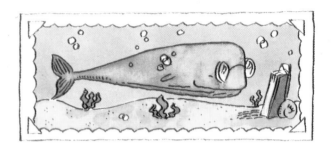

4. What does Brent mean?

I don't need to measure the other sides of the square to find the perimeter.

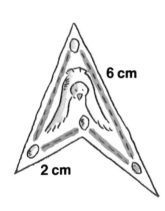

5. Which two sides must Annie measure? Why is this possible?

I only have to measure 2 sides of a rectangle to find the perimeter.

6. Is there enough information to find the perimeter of each decoration without measuring?
If so, find it.

6 cm

2 cm

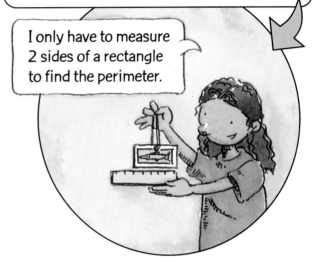

4.5 cm

7 cm

2.5 cm

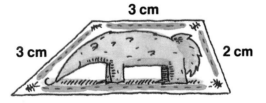

3 cm

3 cm

2 cm

7. Design 3 different quadrilateral ornaments with perimeters of 20 cm.
Explain what you did.

193

Designing Patios

Estimating and Calculating Area in Non-Standard Units

Jaleel's group is designing patios in the shapes of quadrilaterals. Then they find the area or the amount of each surface.

How does Jaleel know this area is 6 square units?

The area is 6 square units.

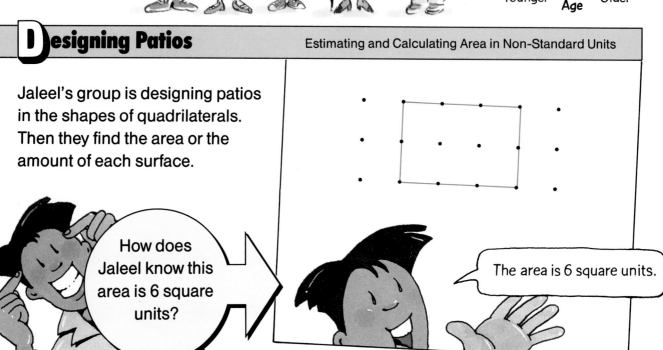

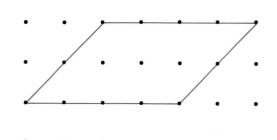

1. The smaller triangle is half of 1 square. The larger triangle is half of 2 squares. What is the area of each triangle? the whole quadrilateral?

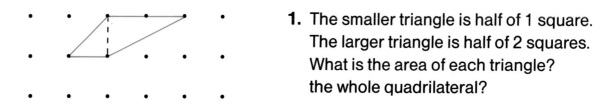

2. Explain why the area of this patio is 8 square units.

3. Model a patio in the shape of a trapezoid with an area of 8 square units.

194

4. What type of quadrilateral is each patio?
Estimate
  · which has the greatest area
  · which has the least area
  · which two have the closest areas

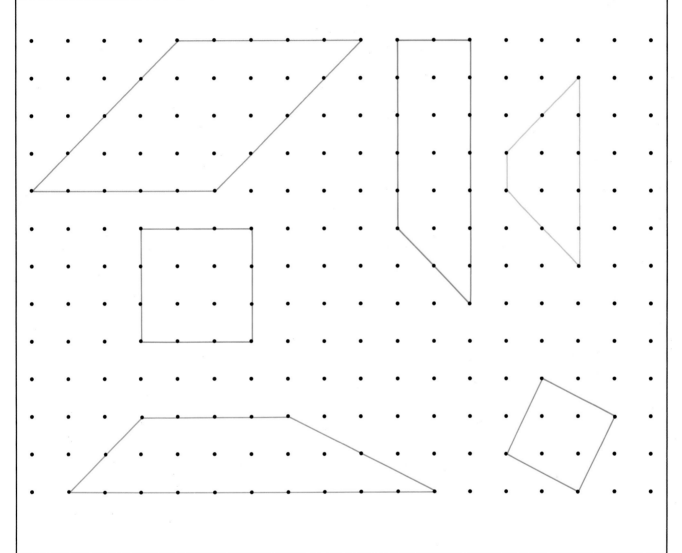

5. Find the area of each. Check your estimates.

6. Which area was the easiest to find? Explain.

7. Use a geoboard to model a patio in each shape with an area
of 10 square units.
  · a rectangle   · a trapezoid   · a parallelogram

Use your head. Which are less than 1000?
Tell what you did.

101 × 9   737 + 373   3609 − 2598

585 + 385   7225 ÷ 8

 aking Designs

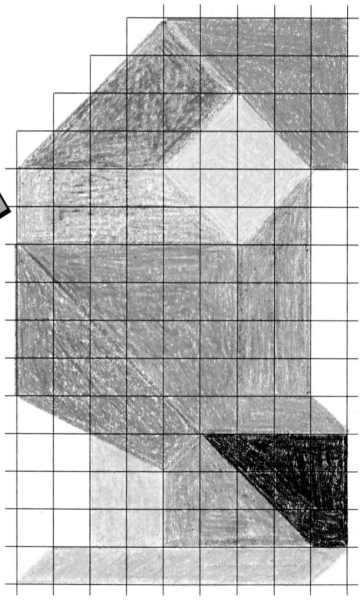

Zoe and Nathan made this
using only quadrilaterals.
Each small square is 1 cm^2
(square centimetre).
How many square centimetres
is the yellow square?

Work with a partner.

1. Estimate which quadrilateral has
   - the greatest area
   - the least area

2. What is the area of the
   whole design?

Use centimetre grid paper.

3. Make a design using at least 6 different quadrilaterals.
   What is its area?
   Write 3 area questions about your design for another pair to answer.

Take Your Pick

SHORT CUTS

Nadine said that to find the perimeter of a square you only need to measure one side. Explain.
How many sides must you measure to find the perimeter of a parallelogram? a rectangle? a rhombus? a kite? a trapezoid?

WHAT CAN YOU MAKE?

Use 4 straws that have lengths of 12 cm, 12 cm, 6 cm, and 6 cm. Make several different quadrilaterals using the straws as sides. How are they alike? different?

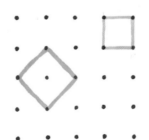

SAME OR DIFFERENT?

Explain why the parallelogram and the rectangle have the same area.

How could you make a trapezoid with the same area?

MAKING SQUARES

How many different-sized squares can you make on a geoboard like this?

PUZZLING PARALLELOGRAMS

Create two parallelograms on a geoboard or dot paper. The one with the lesser perimeter should have the greater area.

Make up other problems. Post them on the bulletin board for your classmates to solve.

197

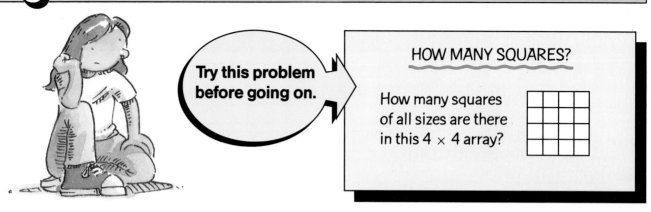

Try this problem before going on.

HOW MANY SQUARES?

How many squares of all sizes are there in this 4 × 4 array?

Josh's group solved the problem by solving a simpler problem.

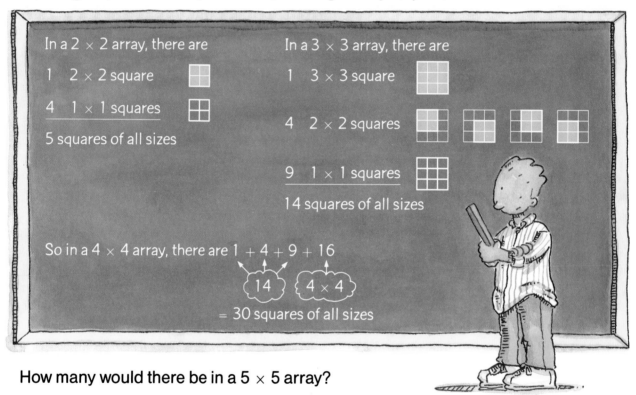

In a 2 × 2 array, there are

1   2 × 2 square

4   1 × 1 squares

5 squares of all sizes

In a 3 × 3 array, there are

1   3 × 3 square

4   2 × 2 squares

9   1 × 1 squares

14 squares of all sizes

So in a 4 × 4 array, there are 1 + 4 + 9 + 16

(14)   (4 × 4)

= 30 squares of all sizes

How many would there be in a 5 × 5 array?

Work in a group.   **Solve these problems by solving a simpler problem.**

HOW MANY TRIANGLES?

How many triangles of all sizes are there here?

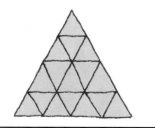

HANGING PICTURES

16 square pictures, all the same size, are hung with a tack in each corner. What is the fewest number of tacks needed?

LOTS OF SEVENS

What is the ones digit of the product when 20 sevens are multiplied together?

I call them beauty marks.

1. Trace these dots.

Use any of them as corners to draw each of these.
- a rectangle
- a rhombus
- a trapezoid

2. Name each type of quadrilateral in this pattern.

3. What is the perimeter of the large kite? a large rectangle? a square?

4. Which of the quadrilaterals do not have at least one line of symmetry?

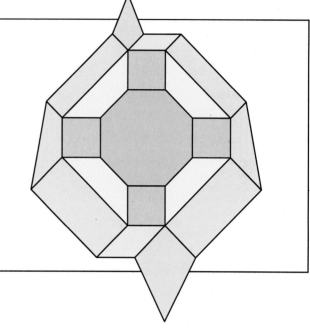

5. Draw a trapezoid that doesn't have a line of symmetry.

6. Use 24 square tiles. How many different rectangles can you make with areas of 24 square units?

7. Describe or identify a solid with each number of square faces.

6   1   2

8. Bina wants to put a fence around the edge of her garden. Fencing costs $5 for each metre. How much will it cost to fence the garden?

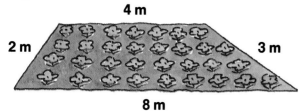

4 m

2 m   3 m

8 m

9. What is the area of this quadrilateral?

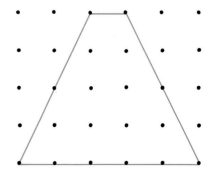

199

Playing Games for Practice

Play each game in a group of 2, 3, or 4.

Just Stretch

- Place an elastic on a geoboard near the centre to make a small parallelogram.
- Shuffle the cards. Place them face down in a pile.
- Turn over the top card. Change the shape to fit the rule on the card. Even if the shape already fits the rule, you must change it.
- Your score is the number of corners you changed.
- Take turns. Play five rounds.
- The winner is the player with the lowest score.

Example

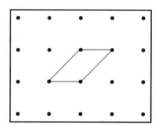

No line of symmetry

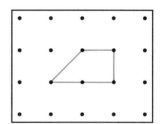

Score 1 point.

Three in a Row

- Roll 2 dice. Use those 2 numbers as the length and width of a rectangle.
- Draw your rectangle on grid paper.
- Find its perimeter and area.
- Place a marker on the number of the perimeter or the area if it is shown on the gameboard.
- Take turns. Use a different color of marker for each player.
- The winner is the first to get 3 in a row.

Example

 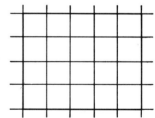

perimeter = 18 units
area = 20 square units

Cover 18.

15	6	8
18	7	12
22	10	14

DESIGNS

Make a design that belongs with these. Explain why it belongs.

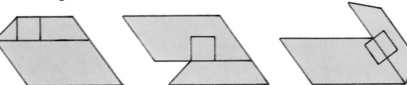

DIVIDE A SQUARE

This square is divided into six smaller squares of two sizes.

Divide a square another way to create smaller squares of two or more sizes.

MIDPOINTS

Draw any quadrilateral.
Mark the midpoint of each side.
Then join those four points.
What type of quadrilateral is formed?

Do this for three other quadrilaterals. What do you notice?

MINI-TRAPEZOIDS

This trapezoid is divided into smaller trapezoids.
Can you always divide trapezoids into smaller ones?
Explain.

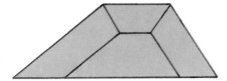

MULTI-TRAPEZOIDS

How many trapezoids are there?

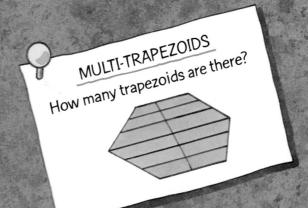

Make up other problems. Post them on the bulletin board for your classmates to solve.

1.

> A square is also a parallelogram.

Is Sam right? Explain.

2. Draw a trapezoid with at least one square corner.
Can a trapezoid have only one square corner? more than two square corners?

3. Which solid can you make with only rectangles? Sketch it and its net. How many faces are there? edges? corners?

4. Use dot paper. Draw two rectangles with the same perimeter but different areas.

5. One side of a rectangle is 8 cm long. The perimeter is 38 cm. What are the lengths of the other sides?

6. Trace this rhombus. Divide it into fourths three different ways. Which of the fourths are quadrilaterals?

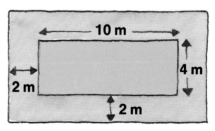

7. Two corners of a rectangle are shown. What ordered pairs name the other two corners?

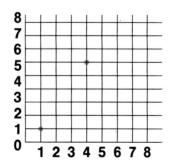

8. A rectangular pool is surrounded by a cement patio that is 2 m wide. The patio is surrounded by a fence. How many metres of fence are there?

9. Use dot paper. Draw a quadrilateral that is not a parallelogram but has two sides the same length.

10. Draw a quadrilateral with an area of 15 half square units on dot paper.

Write a story to tell what the world would be like if no square shapes were allowed.

Where do you find squares in the world outside your classroom?

We find many squares as well as other rectangles in the world but fewer other parallelograms.
Write a paragraph to explain this.

Explain to a friend the difference between perimeter and area.

Draw your favorite quadrilateral. Then explain why it is your favorite.

What questions do you still have about quadrilaterals?

Exploring Mass,

▼ Show how to remove the objects without changing the balance.
How many paper clips are needed to balance 1 eraser?

▼ Which box is heavier? Why?
Tell what might be in each box.

Capacity and Volume

Could these containers hold ▶
the same amount of water?
Tell what you could do to
find out.

◀ 100 chalkboard brushes fill a box.
About how many erasers would you
need to fill the same box?

◀ Write about the different
ways you can measure
one of these.

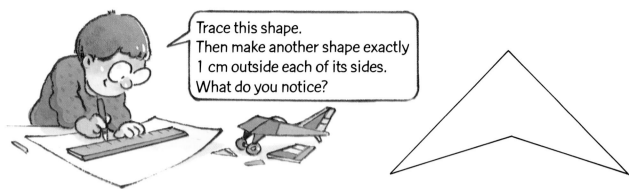

Trace this shape.
Then make another shape exactly
1 cm outside each of its sides.
What do you notice?

Buying Food by Mass

Scales can be used to find mass.

Some labels show the mass.

1. Tell what the numbers and symbols mean.

2. What is the mass of each food? Which is heavier than 1 kg?

Work in a group.

3. List some foods that have labels to show the mass.

4. List some foods for which scales are used to find the mass.

206

Use balance scales, lifting, or the labels.

5. Which of these foods might be in each bag?

Cereal 425 g

WHOLE WHEAT 675 g

215 g

Greater than 900 g

Between 200 g and 600 g

Almost 900 g

6. Pack a bag with foods which have these masses.
- greater than 300 g
- less than 5 g
- about 500 g
- about 1 kg
- greater than 2 kg

Tell what you did to find the masses.

7. Would it be easier to buy food with a mass greater than 1 kg or less than 1 g? Tell why.

8. What is the greatest number of grams you usually see on food labels? Why?

9. When these groceries are packed in a box, is the mass more likely to be greater or less than 20 kg? Explain.

A palindrome is a number that reads the same backwards as forwards. 919 is a palindrome. What numbers less than 300 are palindromes?

Estimating How Heavy

Angela is filling a customer's order for 500 g of ham. She estimated and measured 3 times.

1. How close is each of Angela's estimates to 500 g?

2. Why do you think her estimates get closer each time?

3. Why might she stop estimating after she measured 497 g?

Work in a group.

4. Estimate the amount of seeds, beans, pasta, or rice needed for each bag. Check how close you are each time.

 50 g   100 g   200 g   250 g

5. Estimate the amount of Plasticine needed to make a 100 g Plasticine sausage.
Use Angela's method to make one very close to 100 g.
Use that information to make a sausage with each mass.

25 g   75 g   200 g

Tell what you did.

6. Estimate the mass of 1 L of water.
How did you estimate?
Measure to find the mass.
Use this information to estimate the mass of water each container would hold.
Check how close you are each time.

7. How would you estimate any 3 of these masses?
  • a box holding all the math books in the class
  • a pencil about 1 m long
  • 1000 dried beans
  • 10 000 sheets of photocopy paper
  • a box containing all your classmates' shoes
  • 50 000 staples
  • an object of your choice

8. When is an estimated mass appropriate?
When is an exact mass important?

How many toothpicks would be in the 8th design in this pattern?

Turning into Gold

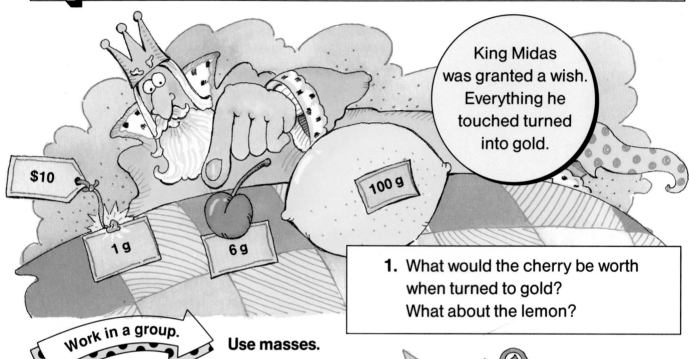

King Midas was granted a wish. Everything he touched turned into gold.

$10

1 g

6 g

100 g

1. What would the cherry be worth when turned to gold? What about the lemon?

Work in a group. Use masses.

2. How many grams of gold nuggets have the same mass as a 1 kg gold bar?

3. What is the value of the bag of nuggets? the gold bar?

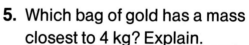

Nuggets [?] g

1 kg

4. How many bags of gold coins would you trade for a 1 kg gold bar?

Coins 250 g

5. Which bag of gold has a mass closest to 4 kg? Explain.

Gold dust 3900 g

Gold coins 3500 g

Gold nuggets 4015 g

6. About how much would a 1.5 kg gold bar be worth?

7. Choose an object. Estimate its value if it was turned into gold.

210

GROWING LIKE A BABY

Your mass at birth probably tripled by your first birthday.
Estimate what your mass would be in 3 years if you started to grow like a baby.
In how many years would you be heavier than the elephant?

7500 kg

SOAKING BEANS

Do dried beans soak up more than their own mass of water?
Which beans soak up the most water?

BIG SQUASH

About how many students do you need to balance the world record squash?
Tell what you did to estimate.

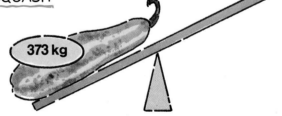

373 kg

PRICEY SPICE

Estimate the cost of 1 kg of saffron.
Tell what you did.
Find out what saffron is and how it is used.

0.5 g Saffron $2.00

$100 OR $1000

Is your mass closer to the mass of $100 of pennies or $1000 of pennies?
How do you know?

Make up other problems. Post them on the bulletin board for your classmates to solve.

Lorne used a milk carton to make this design.
What did he do?

Make another design using a milk carton
or another container.

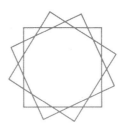

Comparing Containers

The capacity of a container is how much it holds.
These containers have their capacities on their labels.

1. What do the contents of the containers have in common?

2. Tell what you notice about the numbers and the symbols.

3. What do the symbols L and mL stand for?

Work in a group.

**Use containers and pouring materials
to measure when necessary.**

Hmm..?

4. Which size of container in each pair holds more?
   Tell what you did to find out.

   750 mL or 355 mL   1 L or 4 L

   4 L or 1.5 L   250 mL or 1 L

   750 mL or 1 L   3.5 L or 350 mL

212

5. What size of container would you use to make juice from frozen concentrate? Why?

Add 3 cans of water.

6. How can the information on the labels help you choose these containers?
- one with about twice the capacity of another
- one over 4 times the capacity of another
- two different ones that can be filled almost exactly by another one

Check your choices by pouring.

7. Use labelled containers to measure the capacity of each of these unlabelled containers.

- a bucket
- a drinking glass
- a bowl
- a spoon
- a container of your choice

Which are best measured in litres? in millilitres? Explain.

8. What is the greatest number showing capacity that you can find on a container? Why?

9. Is a new bottle of pop completely full? Why or why not? What about other containers?

How could you find the centre of
a square cracker?
a rectangular cracker?
a hexagonal cracker?

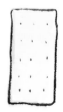

Making Popcorn

Mike and Tammy found that a small amount of kernels made a lot of popcorn.

1 L   2 L

1. How many millilitres of kernels did Tammy and Mike each use?
   About how many litres of popcorn did they each make?
   Why might the amounts they made be different?

Work in a group.   **Use popcorn, measuring cups, and containers.**

2. Estimate how much popcorn they
   might get by popping these
   amounts of kernels.
   200 mL   300 mL   250 mL

3. About how many millilitres of kernels
   should they each use to get about
   10 L of popcorn?

4. Estimate how many litres of popcorn might be made from this jar of kernels.
Tell what you did to estimate.

5. Estimate how much popcorn to put in a bag to show each amount.
Measure to check your estimates.

1 L	500 mL	250 mL
2 L	1.5 L	1500 mL

6. Estimate and then measure how many millilitres of popcorn you can pick up with
• one hand
• both hands

7. Estimate and then measure how many single handfuls of popcorn are needed to fill or empty a 1 L container.

8. Estimate how many litres of popcorn would be needed for every student in the class.
About how many millilitres of popcorn kernels would be needed?

9. Popcorn kernels over 7000 years old have been found.
How do you think people discovered how to pop corn?

Is the perimeter 8 cm?
Measure to find out.

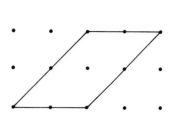

Pouring Pop

Relating Litres and Millilitres

Cindy and Alex's class is selling glasses of pop at the school concert.

1. About how many millilitres of pop have already been poured from the bottle?

2. About how many litres are left in the bottle?

3. How many glasses can be filled from a 2 L bottle?

 **Use containers and pouring material.**

4. Estimate how many times each amount can be poured from a 2 L bottle. Measure to check.
   100 mL   200 mL
   355 mL   750 mL

5. Order these sizes of containers from least to greatest capacity.
   2 L   500 mL   1 L
   750 mL   355 mL   1.5 mL

6. About how many bottles do you need to have the same amount as in a case of 12 cans?

7. At what price should they sell each glass of pop if they want to make money?
   What information did you need?

216

Take Your Pick

INDIVIDUAL SERVING

About how many ketchup packets are needed to have the same amount as in this bottle?

HEAPING SPOONS

How many times as great as a level spoonful is a heaping spoonful?

SCOOPING ICE CREAM

Estimate how many scoops of ice cream you can get from a 2 L container of ice cream. Tell what you did.

JUMBO JELLY

About how many bowls of jelly could be served from this?

World's Largest Jelly
35 000 L

SOAK UP

How much water can a paper towel soak up? What about a sponge? Tell what you did to find out.

Make up other problems. Post them on the bulletin board for your classmates to solve.

Find three ways to make this statement equal about 400. Each time two numbers must be greater than 100 and two must be less than 100.

$$\boxed{?} \times \boxed{?} + \boxed{?} - \boxed{?}$$

Stacking Rods

Robert stacked 18 rods like this.

The volume or the amount of space taken by the stack is 18 rods.

Show a volume of 18 rods some other ways.

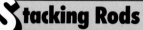

Work in a group.

Use base ten blocks.

1. Which stacks of rods have the same volume?

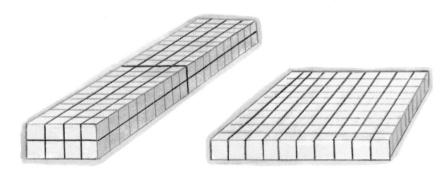

2. These are the top layers of stacks with the same volume. How many layers might be in each stack?

 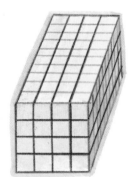

3. Build stacks having a volume between 24 and 30 rods that look like
- a staircase
- a long sidewalk
- a tall building
- a bed

4. Make 2 different stacks of rods having the same volume as
- 1 flat
- 2 flats
- 30 units

Tell how you can be sure your stacks have these volumes.

5. How many rods do you need to build a stack with the same volume as a large cube?
Tell how you know.

6. Estimate how many rods you need to build a model with about the same volume as
- your math book
- a chalkboard eraser
- a 2 L milk carton
- a slice of bread
- a juice box
- an object of your choice

Which objects are easiest to model with rods?

7. Find an object with a volume of about 60 rods.
Did other groups find different objects? Explain.

These are the first four square numbers.
What are the next three?
Why do square numbers alternate between odd and even?

1

4

9

16

Building a Model Town

Niki built a bridge for a model town.

How many cubes did she use to build the bridge? Niki said the volume of her model was 24 cubic centimetres.

She wrote 24 cm³.

1. Why do you think we say each cube has a volume of 1 cm³?

2. How are the symbols cm³ and cm² the same? different?

Work in a group.

Use base ten blocks.

3. Make a building with a volume of 24 cm³.
   Compare its shape to the bridge.
   Compare your building with another group's. Tell what you notice.

4. How many centimetre cubes do you need to make a building with the same volume as a rod? a flat? a large cube?

5. Make 2 models for the town using different combinations of base ten blocks. Find their volumes in cubic centimetres.

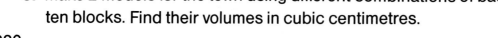

220

Take Your Pick

MILK CUBES

Estimate how many centimetre cubes would fit in an empty 1 L milk carton. Tell what you did.

PACKING BOOKS

Estimate how many math books could be packed into a box.
Tell what you did.
Pack some math books into the box.
Does it make a difference how you pack the books?

BUILDING BOXES

If centimetre grid paper like this was folded and taped to make a box, how many centimetre cubes would fit in it?
Build a box into which exactly 27 centimetre cubes would fit.

ESTIMATING BOX SIZE

Choose one of these objects.
Estimate the size of box needed to pack 12 of them.
Tell how packing these objects is different from packing books.

CRAYON BOXES

Describe the ways that crayons are packed in boxes.
How many crayons do you usually see in a box?
Tell why you will probably never buy a box of 29 crayons.

Make up other problems. Post them on the bulletin board for your classmates to solve.

221

Try this problem before going on.

SOAKING WET

What amount of water can be picked up by a bath towel?

Kali's group solved the problem by planning and doing an experiment.

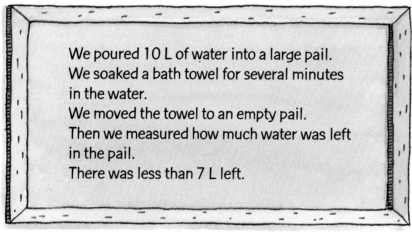

We poured 10 L of water into a large pail.
We soaked a bath towel for several minutes in the water.
We moved the towel to an empty pail.
Then we measured how much water was left in the pail.
There was less than 7 L left.

About how much did the bath towel soak up?

Work in a group.

Solve these problems by planning and doing experiments.

DRAWING UP WATER

How high can you draw water up into a straw without putting the straw to your mouth?

DRIP, DROP, DRIP

How much water is wasted in 1 week by a dripping tap?

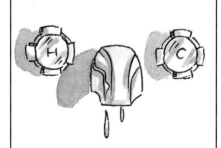

LEFT-OVER SPACE

Which leaves the greatest amount of space for water?

Sand   Marbles   Gravel

1. Which mass is closest to 1 kg? Explain.

   2000 g   1455 g   10 001 g   975 g

2. Which container has the greatest capacity? Explain.

3. What can be bought that is measured in grams? kilograms? litres? millilitres?

4. Which two masses can be put together to make a mass heavier than 1 kg?

   100 g   454 g   500 g   750 g

5. Tell whether litres or millilitres should be used to measure the capacity of each container.

6. From which size of container would you most likely drink?

   50 mL   350 mL   1.5 L

7. Estimate whether your math textbook is heavier or lighter than 100 g.

8. Estimate whether the capacity of the classroom waste paper basket is greater or less than 4 L.

9. Would the mass of a hot dog be greater or less than 50 g? Why?

10. What is the volume of each in cans?

Play each game in a group of 2, 3, or 4.

Greatest Mass

- Shuffle the cards. Place them face down in a pile.
- Take turns drawing a card from the pile and turning it face up.
- The player with the card showing the greatest mass gets the face-up cards.
- Tied players draw another card to break the tie.
- Play continues until all the cards have been turned up.
- The player with the most cards wins.

Example

 The player who turned up 2 kg gets the cards.

Variation: The player with the least mass gets the cards.

Pour It In

- Shuffle the cards. Place them face down in a pile.
- Turn over the top card. Read the number of millilitres.
- Position an elastic band on a 2 L plastic bottle to estimate how high that many millilitres of pouring material will go.
- Pour some pouring material to the height of the elastic band.
- Then measure this amount in a measuring container.
- Score 3 points for an estimate within 50 mL
  - 2 points for an estimate within 100 mL
  - 1 point for an estimate within 150 mL
- Take 5 turns each. The player with the greatest score is the winner.

Example 750 mL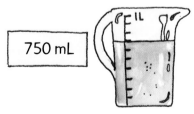

The estimate is within 100 mL.
Score 2 points.

Showing What You Know

1. Two model buildings have volumes of 10 cm³ and 16 cm³.
   Can you tell which is taller? Explain.

2. Why do you not usually find drink containers labelled 2000 mL?

3. Exactly 1 L of water has been poured into each container. Which container would you rather use to estimate the level of 2 L of water? Explain.

4. The average human brain has a mass of 1.36 kg.
   Tell how you know its mass is between 1000 g and 2000 g.

5. Name 6 grocery items sold by mass or capacity where $\frac{1}{3}$ of them are sold by mass.

6. How could you use an empty 1 L milk carton to estimate about 750 mL of water?

7. Name a fruit or vegetable that is longer than 30 cm and has a mass greater than 10 kg.

8. Explain how they both could be right.

The box holds 48 loaves of bread.

The box holds 60 loaves of bread.

9. Tell how to estimate the mass of one bacon slice.

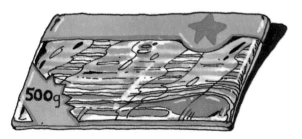

10. Use centimetre cubes to cover a rectangular area of 24 cm². What is the perimeter of the rectangular base?
    If you added two more layers, what would the volume of your rectangular solid be?

225

Each label is from a container.
Act out how you would hold and move each container.
Tell what might be in each.

Tell what *kilo* means
in the word *kilogram*.
What other measurements
do you know that use *kilo*?
Tell what you think *kilolitre*
might mean.
Do you think you can buy a drink
in a kilolitre container?

I need one box please.

What questions would you ask
the man before choosing a box?

Is 500 mL a reasonable estimate
for the capacity of this container?
Tell why or why not.

Explain why both might be right.

5 kg - not nearly enough!

5 kg - way too much!

**What questions do
you still have about
mass, capacity, and
volume?**

Investigating Climate and Weather

How do you think these students are measuring rainfall?

What is your weather like today?

What do you think the chance is tomorrow of having sunshine? rain? snow?

How would you describe the climate where you live?

WHAT Do Temperature Graphs Tell Us?

In Winnipeg, the average temperature in July was 20°C or 20 degrees Celsius.
The average temperature in November was −5°C or minus 5 degrees Celsius.

Average Temperatures in Winnipeg

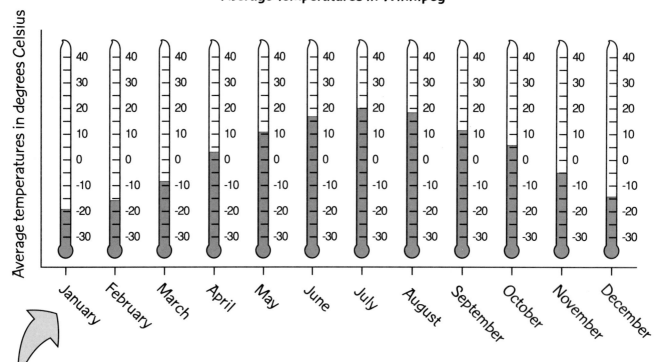

Average temperatures in degrees Celsius

January   February   March   April   May   June   July   August   September   October   November   December

1. Which months have an average temperature below freezing? Choose 2 months and find the difference in average temperatures. Which 2 months have the greatest difference in temperature?

2. Predict the order of the months from coldest to hottest in Winnipeg. Then list the months in order from least to greatest average temperature.

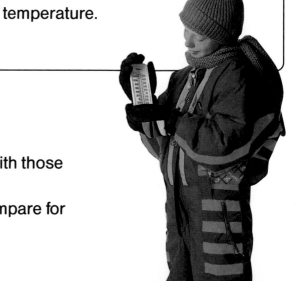

Work in a group.

3. Compare the temperatures on the graph with those where you live for the first 6 months. How do you think the temperatures will compare for the last 6 months?

228

4. Each hour, estimate the temperature outside your school and then use a thermometer. Record the temperatures in a table.

Time	Temperature	
	Estimate	Actual
9:10	20°C	19°C
10:10	19°C	23°C

5. Color a picture of a thermometer to show each temperature. Arrange the thermometers as a bar graph.

6. What is the average temperature? Draw a line across your graph to show it.
How many degrees altogether do the bars reach above the line? fall below the line?

7. Did temperatures change during the day? Why? Estimate temperatures halfway between times on the graph. Do you think these estimates could be the exact temperatures?

8. Predict temperatures for times this evening and during the day tomorrow. Check your predictions later.

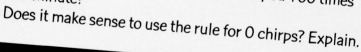

Did You Know...?

You can estimate the temperature in degrees Celsius by counting the chirps made by the American tree cricket. You count the number of chirps in 1 minute. Then divide the number by 8 and add 6.

▶ What is the temperature if a cricket chirped 160 times in 1 minute?
Does it make sense to use the rule for 0 chirps? Explain.

WHAT Do Precipitation Records Tell Us?

Precipitation means rain, snow, sleet, or hail.
Temperatures must be above 0°C for rain and
below 0°C for snow.

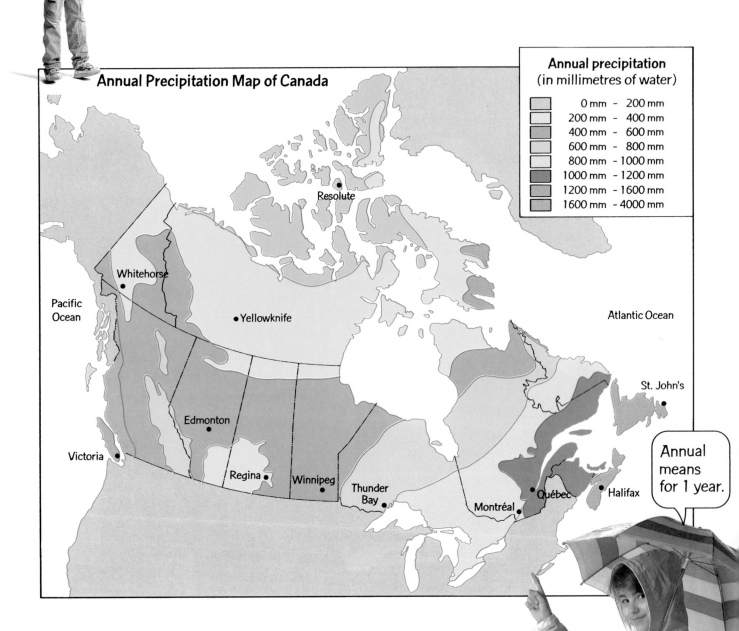

Annual Precipitation Map of Canada

Annual precipitation
(in millimetres of water)

	0 mm – 200 mm
	200 mm – 400 mm
	400 mm – 600 mm
	600 mm – 800 mm
	800 mm – 1000 mm
	1000 mm – 1200 mm
	1200 mm – 1600 mm
	1600 mm – 4000 mm

Resolute

Pacific
Ocean

Whitehorse

Yellowknife

Atlantic Ocean

St. John's

Edmonton

Victoria

Regina

Winnipeg

Thunder
Bay

Montréal

Québec

Halifax

Annual
means
for 1 year.

1. Use the map to find the annual precipitation for your area.
   How high in your classroom would this reach if it was all rain?

2. If the precipitation was all snow, it would be about 10 times as high.
   About how high would this reach?

3. About how much rain do you think falls in your area in a year?
   About how much snow?

230

Use the map.

4. Record the high and low annual precipitation for your area and for 4 cities in different colored areas.
   Order the 5 places from the least to the greatest precipitation.
   Why do you think the precipitation varies?

5. Use the high annual precipitation you recorded for your area.
   What is the average for each month?
   How does the average compare with your weather last month?
   Repeat this for the low precipitation for your area.
   Predict the precipitation in millimetres for next month.

Use the photo.

6. Both rain gauges show that 20 mm of rain fell during 1 hour of heavy rainfall. Why is the water level higher in the second container?

7. Estimate the amount of rainfall if the rain fell like this for $2\frac{1}{2}$ hours.
   About how many rainy days like this would it take to have 1 m of rain?

Did You Know...?

In Lakeland, B.C., 118 cm of snow fell in 1 day!

▶ Estimate how high on your body the snow would reach. How many days like this would it take for the snow to be as high as your school?

HOW Is Wind Measured?

This scale describes the speed of the wind.

Beaufort number	Name of wind	Effects of the wind	Kilometres per hour
0	Calm	Smoke rises straight up.	Less than 1
1	Light air	Smoke drifts gently. Weather vane is still.	1-5
2	Light breeze	Face feels wind. Leaves rustle.	6-11
3	Gentle breeze	Leaves and small twigs move.	12-19
4	Moderate breeze	Dust, paper, and small branches move.	20-28
5	Fresh breeze	Small trees sway. Wavelets form on lakes.	29-38
6	Strong breeze	Branches move. Wind is heard in wires.	39-49
7	Moderate gale	Whole trees move. Walking is difficult.	50-61
8	Fresh gale	Twigs are broken off.	62-74
9	Strong gale	Loose shingles and chimneys are blown off.	75-88
10	Whole gale	Trees are uprooted.	89-102
11	Storm	Widespread damage occurs.	103-117
12	Hurricane	Anything may be damaged or destroyed.	Above 117

Work in a group.

1. Predict the speed of the wind
   • in the photo
   • outside your school today

Wind is described by the direction it is blowing from.

2. Make a weather vane like this to find wind direction.

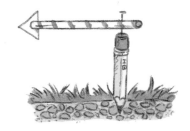

Cut one end of a straw.
Put a cardboard arrow into the cut.
Pin the straw into the eraser of a pencil.
Push the pencil into the ground.
Draw a compass around the pencil.

3. In what direction will the weather vane point with a north wind? south wind? east wind? west wind?

4. Make an anemometer like this to measure wind speed.

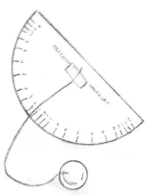

Glue a scale on half a circle of cardboard.

Use about 30 cm of thread to attach a ping pong ball to the cardboard.

Why do you think 0 kilometres per hour is placed where it is?
Why do you think the anemometer needs to be kept level when measuring wind speed?
Where would the ball and string be in winds greater than 60 kilometres per hour?

5. Use your instruments to find the speed and direction of the wind outside your school each hour. Record this information in a table.

6. Order the times in your table from windiest to least windy.
Estimate the wind speed and direction for the windiest time yesterday.
Predict the wind speed and direction for the windiest time tomorrow.
Why do you think it is important to know the speed and direction of wind?

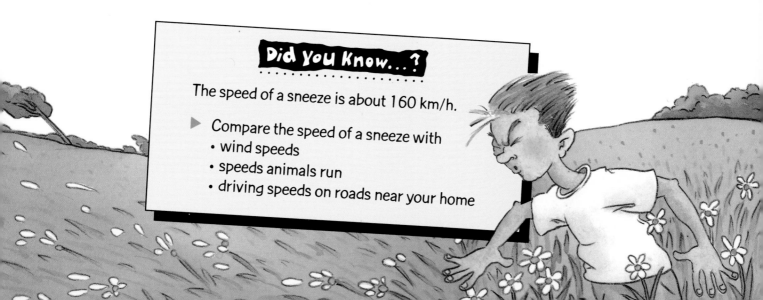

Did you know...?

The speed of a sneeze is about 160 km/h.

▶ Compare the speed of a sneeze with
  • wind speeds
  • speeds animals run
  • driving speeds on roads near your home

? I Wonder... ?

Weather Wise

Red sky at night, sailors' delight.
Red sky in the morning, sailors' warning.

Does the rhyme make sense?
Record red skies and the weather on a calendar for several days
to find out.

Cloudy Skies

Does a cloudy sky at night affect the temperature the next day?
Record cloud cover at night and temperatures the next day on a
calendar for several days to find out.

Sunrise and Sunset

What are the times this week for sunrise and sunset?
How much difference is there each day in sunrise time?
sunset time? amount of daylight?
Are the hours of daylight getting less or greater?
Is this true for other months of the year?

Visiting America

Temperature in the United States
is reported in degrees Fahrenheit
and not in degrees Celsius, as in
Canada.

°F	80	70	60	50	?	?	?
°C	27	21	16	10	?	?	?

Is there a pattern?
What other temperatures belong
in the table?
What are the freezing and boiling
points?

Chinooks

What are chinooks?
Where are chinooks?
How can numbers
be used to describe
chinooks?

**Make up your OWN investigation.
Then post it on the bulletin board
for others to try.**

Write a weather forecast for a day next week.
What would you include in the forecast?
What temperatures are reasonable?

Use measurements to describe the hottest day, the coldest day, the windiest day, the rainiest day, and the snowiest day you remember. Use numbers in your descriptions.

Compare the temperature, precipitation, and wind in your area with those in another part of Canada.

Which would you like better?
Why?

Rainfall in millimetres

15
10
5
0

Sun. Mon. Tues. Wed. Thurs. Fri. Sat.

Explain the graph.
Write and answer a question comparing the rainfall on 2 days.
What month do you think this might be for your area?

What else would you like to know about weather and climate?
Tell what you would do to find out.

Index